GLOBETROTTER™

Travel Guide

CORFU

MIKE GERRARD

D1334065

HOLLAND

NEW
HOLLAND

★★★ Highly recommended
★★ Recommended
★ See if you can

Sixth edition published in 2009
by New Holland Publishers (UK) Ltd
London • Cape Town • Sydney • Auckland
10 9 8 7 6 5 4 3
website: www.newhollandpublishers.com

Garfield House,
86 Edgware Road
London W2 2EA, United Kingdom

80 McKenzie Street
Cape Town 8001, South Africa

Unit 1, 66 Gibbes Street,
Chatswood NSW 2067, Australia

218 Lake Road
Northcote, Auckland, New Zealand

Distributed in the USA by
The Globe Pequot Press, Connecticut

Copyright © 2009 in text: Mike Gerrard
Copyright © 2009 in maps: Globetrotter Travel Maps
Copyright © 2009 in photographs:
Individual photographers as credited (right)
Copyright © 2009 New Holland Publishers (UK) Ltd

ISBN 978 1 84773 394 8

This guidebook has been written by independent authors
and updaters. The information therein represents their
impartial opinion, and neither they nor the publishers
accept payment in return for including in the book or
writing more favourable reviews of any of the establishments. Whilst every effort has been made to ensure that
this guidebook is as accurate and up to date as possible,
please be aware that the facts quoted are subject to
change, particularly the price of food, transport and
accommodation. The Publisher accepts no responsibility
or liability for any loss, injury or inconvenience incurred
by readers or travellers using this guide.

Publishing Manager: Thea Grobbelaar
DTP Cartographic Manager: Genené Hart

Editors: Lorissa Bouwer, Carla Zietsman, Melany
McCallum, Thea Grobbelaar, Mary Duncan, Audrey Horne
Cartographers: Inga Ndibongo, Reneé Spocter,
Nicole Bannister
Design and DTP: Nicole Bannister, Philip Mann, ACE Ltd
Picture Researcher: Felicia Apollis
Consultant: Judith Hampson

Reproduction by Hirt & Carter (Pty) Ltd, Cape Town.
Printed and bound by Times Offset (M) Sdn. Bhd., Malaysia.

Photographic Credits: David Alexander, pages 4, 6, 97, 106,
109, 114, 117; **Jeanetta Baker**, pages 65 (bottom), 98, 111;
Peter Baker, pages 19, 26, 30, 41, 55, 63, 67, 74, 82, 87, 92;
Mike Gerrard pages 14, 15, 17, 18, 29, 33, 35, 38, 39, 40,
42, 46, 47, 48, 49, 50, 51, 52, 119, 120; **George Grigoriou/
Tony Stone Images/Gallo Images**, title page; **Robert Harding**,
pages 25, 101; **Robert Harding/Martyn F. Chillmaid**, page 9;
Robert Harding/Andy Williams, page 103; **Terry Harris**,
pages 24, 27, 28, 85, 110; **Roger Howard**, pages 8, 16, 22,
44, 68, 69, 70, 71, 83, 89; **Gordon Lethbridge**, pages 23, 78,
105; **Alan Lewis**, page 88; **D. M. Littlewood**, pages 54, 73,
81, 90, 100, 104; **Julie Meech**, page 10; **Pictures Colour
Library**, pages 21, 37, 43; **Prittipix**, pages 11, 99; **Sime/Photo
Access**, cover; **Spectrum Colour Library**, pages 13, 95; **Peter
Whalley**, pages 7, 58, 65 (top), 66.

Keep us Current
Information in travel guides is apt to change, which is why
we regularly update our guides. We'd be grateful to receive
feedback if you've noted something we should include in
our updates. If you have new information, please share it
with us by writing to the Publishing Manager, Globetrotter,
at the office nearest to you (addresses on this page). The
most significant contribution to each new edition will
receive a free copy of the updated guide.

Note:
In the transliteration of place names from Greek to English
spellings, various authors have tried to convey Greek sounds
in different ways. The Greek gamma is not a simple 'g' but is
more gutteral or can have a 'y' sound. Thus many different
spellings are encountered. For example, *Agios*, meaning
'saint' and used in all church names (e.g. Agios Yioryiou),
can also be spelt *Aghios* or *Ayios*. Similarly 'dh' is sometimes
used to convey the soft 'th' sound of a Greek delta – elsewhere you might find a simple 'd'. To avoid confusion, all
accents have been omitted from the place names in this guide.

Cover: *Paleokastritsa Bay.*
Title page: *Paleokastritsa, northwest Corfu.*

CONTENTS

1
Introducing
Corfu (Kerkyra)

Visitors and settlers have been delighted by the green and pleasant island of Corfu for thousands of years. It was already a popular holiday destination in Roman times, and today it is one of the busiest spots in the Mediterranean.

Corfu (Kerkyra) has a population of about 113,000 packed into its 593km² (229 sq miles), making it one of the most densely populated parts of Greece – and that's without the annual impact of almost one million visitors. Nevertheless, such figures are misleading, as over one-third of the population lives in the capital, Corfu Town. There is some 217km (135 miles) of glorious coastline for visitors to enjoy, and the vast majority of these shoehorn themselves into a handful of bustling seaside resorts, so escape from the crowds is still possible. And though few coastal villages are totally untouched by tourism, some have not yet been taken over by it.

What has made Corfu so popular? For one thing, it can boast some of the best **beaches** in Greece. Its climate is **warm** for most of the year and regular rainfall makes Corfu an unusually green Mediterranean island. The **scenery** is outstanding, with the north dominated by the majestic slopes of Mount Pantokrator, and the **people** possess the traditional Greek friendliness (in Greek the word for 'stranger' and 'guest' is the same). Inland are **hillside and mountain villages** where life goes on much as it must have done a hundred or even a thousand years ago. And finally, **Corfu Town** is probably the most attractive capital to be found in any of the Greek islands.

TOP ATTRACTIONS

★★★ Paleokastritsa: a cluster of bays and beaches, one of the most scenic spots in all Greece.
★★★ Mount Pantokrator: Corfu's highest peak, with unrivalled views all around.
★★★ Mouse Island: Corfu's most photographed sight.
★★ The Liston: Corfu Town's arcaded street of cafés.
★★ The Old Town: a labyrinth of narrow streets in Corfu Town.
★★ Museum of Asiatic Art: a unique oriental collection in Corfu Town.

Opposite: *This peaceful scene at Pontikonissi greets travellers arriving by air.*

WHAT'S IN A NAME?

The Greek name for Corfu is Kerkyra. According to one tradition this derives from a nymph named Kerkyra or Korkyra, brought to the island by the sea god Poseidon who was in love with her. Another possible derivation is from the Greek kerkos, meaning 'handle', referring to the island's shape. Corfu has also been known as Drepanon or Drepani, meaning 'sickle'. The English name Corfu probably comes from the Greek word korifai (peaks), as a twin-peaked citadel once stood on the site of Corfu Town. The name was corrupted into Corfu by European settlers, and this is now how most of the inhabitants refer to the island themselves.

THE LAND

The most northerly of the seven Ionian Islands, Corfu measures just 58km (36 miles) lengthwise and 27km (17 miles) across at its widest point. From north to south it is shaped like a handle or a sickle, a form reflected in past names for the island in Greek. It can be roughly divided into three main areas: the **mountainous north**, the **hilly centre** and the more **low-lying south**. Much of the coast is sandy or pebbly, giving beautiful long stretches of **beach**, particularly to the west of the Antinioti Lagoon on the north coast, and along Lake Korission in the southwest. There are also lengthy expanses of **cliffs**, especially on the west coast to the north of the holiday resort of Ermones. A series of unusual low cliffs spectacularly striped with layers of clay and sand can be seen at Sidari and Peroulades in the north.

North Corfu is dominated by the peak of **Mount Pantokrator**, rising to 906m (2973ft) and sometimes lightly capped with snow in winter. Corfu's wet, warm climate ensures that the slopes are thickly carpeted with a wide variety of flowers in the spring, notably many species of orchid. From the mountain's summit to the nearest beach resorts, such as Nissaki and Barbati, is less than 3km (2 miles), which gives some idea of how steeply the slopes rise behind these beaches and the spectacular setting provided by the mountain.

Opposite: *The beach and bay at Barbati are typical of the dramatic settings of northern Corfu.*
Right: *There are still far more olive trees than tourists on Corfu, but both provide an annual income for the Corfiots.*

Rivers and Lagoons

While Corfu is too small to have any really large flowing rivers, its regular rainfall means that it is much better watered than almost any other Greek island. There are several small rivers, the most notable being the **Ropa River**, which waters the fertile Ropa Plain in the centre of the island. It also waters Corfu's sole golf course, where its meandering course makes it a hazard at almost every hole. When not distracting golfers, the river irrigates the plain, where vines and cereals grow in abundance.

There are three large lagoons. The **Antinioti Lagoon** on the north coast is in a fairly undeveloped area – though there is one popular beach close by – which means that wildlife can flourish in its waters and surrounding reed beds. By contrast, the **Halikiopoulos Lagoon** to the immediate south of Corfu Town is now the site of the airport runway; despite that, it still serves as home to rare white egrets and families of otters. Egrets can also be found at **Lake Korission** in the south, along with ibis, avocets, orchids ... and Greek hunters. Hunting is as popular on Corfu as on other Mediterranean islands.

BIRD LIFE

Corfu may not be the best spot in the Mediterranean for bird-watching, but for such a small island it offers a great deal of variety to the ornithologist. There are mountain slopes, cypress and olive groves, coastal cliffs and lagoons. The Halikiopoulos Lagoon, within walking distance of Corfu Town, is the winter home of the rare **white egret** as well as the **Dalmatian pelican**. **Audouin's gull** also visits Corfu in winter. Both peregrine and Eleonora's **falcons** inhabit the cliffs, and you can also look out for the **blue rock thrush**. Colourful migrants include **bee-eaters** and the beautiful **golden oriole**.

Right: *Corfu has some of the cleanest waters in the Mediterranean, with beaches safe for bathing.*

Climate

Corfu has a very appealing climate, which is why there are enclaves of people from northern Europe who have settled on the island. In midsummer the temperature will generally be around 31°C (88°F), and the whole island will be comfortably warm from April through to November – in May, the average temperature is about 20°C (68°F). In high summer you can expect 11 or 12 hours of sunshine a day, and even in December there is an average of three hours' sunshine per day. January and February are the coldest months, and there are very occasional frosts and snowfalls.

The island has **regular rainfall**, with the probability of a few showers even in July and August; in fact, Corfu is the wettest place in Greece, with almost as much rainfall as London. This does have its advantages. Corfu is green and fertile, with a wide variety of produce, a good wine-making industry and none of the water-shortage problems experienced by some of the Aegean islands towards the end of their bone-dry summers. July is the driest month, when just a few isolated showers are likely, falling on an average of two days. There is fairly regular rainfall from November through to March, and in October or November there will be a short period of thunderstorms, as the warmer weather finally breaks and gives way to winter.

Wildlife

There is plenty of wild life in Corfu's nightclubs in August – but the island is not short of the natural history variety either. Indeed, it was the richness of its wildlife that enchanted the British zoologist Gerald Durrell, whose boyhood was spent on the island (*see* panel, page 70).

There are rarities, but you need dedication and luck to see them. The seas around Corfu are home to a few of Europe's remaining tiny population of **Mediterranean monk seals**. These animals were mentioned by Homer, but today only about 500 survive. More common – but still endangered – is the **loggerhead turtle**; some can be found around Corfu though they tend to prefer the more southerly Ionian islands. Only the extremely lucky visitor will spot a **jackal**: very few of these wild dogs are left in Europe, but some still carry on their nocturnal lives in the remotest parts of Corfu. You are far more likely to see hares, bats and hedgehogs.

Spring is the best time to visit, when the days are warm, the plantlife is burgeoning and the bird populations are increased by migrant species. There is a rich

THE HERB GARDEN

Corfu is as rich in herbs as it is in every other kind of plant, and local people can often be seen picking these in the hills, or even on unpromising looking sites in towns. To be effective, the herbs have to be gathered on the right Saint's Day. Oregano is picked on 24 June, the feast of St John, while basil must wait till 14 September, the feast of the Holy Cross. Other common herbs include camomile, thyme and sage, this last being made into a tea as well as being used widely in cooking.

Below: *In spring the island is bursting with colour, and visitors are few in number.*

variety of habitat for the wildlife, from meadows and marshes to mountain slopes, lagoons, cliff faces and vast groves of olive and cypress trees. Even in Corfu Town, in the green retreat of the British Cemetery, you will find orchids on the ground and be able to watch for redstarts or goldcrests high in the trees.

Above: *Mount Pantokrator is home to many beautiful flowers such as this* Sternbergia lutea, *known in Greek as the* Krinaki *or* Agriokrinos.

Mount Pantokrator is the big attraction, and is dealt with in more detail in Chapter 3 (page 72), but no naturalist should miss a climb to its summit or the chance to spend a few days exploring its slopes in search of **orchids** or **raptors**. Kestrels are common, but red-footed falcons, Egyptian vultures, buzzards, goshawks, peregrines and golden eagles also occur infrequently. In the olive groves which cover most of the island you will find several varieties of warbler, flycatcher or shrike, and at night you might hear the distinctive bell-like sound of the Scop's owl calling. Probably the most colourful spring visitor is the **bee-eater**, arriving from Africa and unmistakable when it flies into the air from its perch in an explosion of silky greens, blues and golds.

EUROPE'S MOST ENDANGERED MAMMAL

The **Mediterranean monk seal** has been around for 15 million years, but today it is Europe's most endangered mammal. Its relative, the Caribbean monk seal, became extinct in the 1950s. As its name suggests, it is a retiring creature, easily disturbed and easily affected by pollution. There are small numbers of monk seals living in the seas around Corfu. Should you see one you should make no attempt to approach, and if anyone offers you a trip to see seals, politely refuse, explaining why. You should also avoid leaving rubbish in the sea, or on the shore where it can be washed out to sea.

There are **tortoises** too, and several species of **snake** and **lizard**, as well as abundant **butterflies** attracted by the fragrant herbs and plants of Corfu's *maquis* vegetation. Most of the snakes are non-poisonous, and in any case they are adept at getting out of the way when they feel the vibration of human footsteps. The only very venomous snake is the **sand viper**, but this is mainly nocturnal; it is distinctive, having what looks like a horn above each eye. Should you be unlucky enough to be bitten, you must seek medical attention immediately. Most visitors to the island, however, suffer nothing worse than the occasional mosquito bite.

Left: *This chapel is built into the rock of the Byzantine castle of Angelokastro.*

Byzantine Rule

The Byzantine period was a far from peaceful one for the island. **Vandals** sacked Corfu in 455, and out of frustration at not being able to capture the capital they wreaked great havoc on much of the rest of the island. Later, Corfu was caught up in the battles between the Roman forces and the **Goths**; after overrunning Italy, the Goths sacked Corfu in 562 and made it a base from which they could attack parts of the Greek mainland.

In the 11th century, when the **Norman forces** were pushing south, they in their turn sought to seize Corfu as a base, to enable them to extend their territory east-wards into the Balkans. The main attack was initially made by the son of the Norman military leader, **Robert Guiscard**, but Guiscard himself was obliged to enter the fray and helped take the island. He faced a later rebellion when both Byzantine and Venetian ships rallied to the Corfiot cause, but the powerful Norman armies were victorious. The Norman forces were finally vanquished in 1147, again by a joint effort of Corfiot, Byzantine and Venetian troops but other changes were soon to come.

NORMAN CONQUEROR

Robert Guiscard was born in Normandy in the early part of the 11th century, and went to Italy where he eventually became leader of the Normans there. He became an ally of Pope Nicholas II, and went on to capture large parts of the Balkans. He died of fever on Kefallonia in 1085, when he was about 70 years old and still fighting.

When the Byzantine Empire was finally defeated by the Fourth Crusade in 1204, Corfu was put under Venetian rule, but in 1214 the island was invaded yet again, this time by the forces of the Despot of Epirus, **Michael II Angelos Komnenos**. The remains of the fortress of Angelokastro which he built near Paleokastritsa can still be seen. When the Despot was later threatened by the powerful Sicilian king, Manfred, he gave Manfred the hand of his daughter, together with Corfu, as part of the dowry. In 1267 the Pope gave the island to Charles of Anjou, who was also King of Naples, in recognition of his support for the Papacy against the Holy Roman Empire, and it remained under Angevin control for over a hundred years, when the Orthodox church was increasingly repressed.

Venetian Rule (1386–1797)

In 1386 a group of leading Corfiots, anxious for stability after a period of disputed claims to the island, approached the Doge of Venice for protection. The Venetian forces took Corfu by storm, and in 1402 Venice officially claimed it, paying the King of Naples 30,000 gold ducats in compensation. The ensuing four centuries of rule from Venice had many consequences, but two in particular stand out.

Firstly, Corfu was the only part of modern Greece never to fall to **the Turks**, despite vigorous Turkish attempts to occupy it. The Venetians made the island their main arsenal in Greece and built many fortifications, all of which helped the islanders to repel repeated Turkish attacks during the 15th to 18th centuries. These brought intense suffering to the Corfiot population, but the Old Fortress in Corfu Town never succumbed. Given the antagonism that still exists today between the Greeks and the Turks, the Corfiots are proud to be able to claim that their island never fell.

DEATH AND DEFIANCE

In 1537, the infamous pirate-admiral Barbarossa, under the rule of Suleiman the Magnificent, invaded Corfu. He slaughtered the unfortunate inhabitants who had been cruelly locked outside Corfu Town's Old Fortress and burned the entire island before being driven off, taking with him 20,000 Corfiot slaves for sale in Constantinople. Just 34 years later, Sinan Pasha – another thug in the mould of Barbarossa – renewed the Turkish assault and, after three attacks, had literally decimated the island's population. But he failed to take the Old Fortress. In 1716 the Turks returned. After a six-week struggle, when the defenders were apparently about to succumb, the enemy miraculously retreated, due – so the islanders would maintain – to the intervention of St Spiridhon, their patron saint, who raised a violent storm.

A second, much more important and permanent monument to the influence of the Venetians is visible wherever you look on Corfu: **the olive tree**. Although the Venetians did not introduce the tree to the island – they are believed to have grown here for at least 5000 years – they encouraged the farmers to grow them as intensively as possible to meet the tremendous demand for olive oil back in Venice. Other native species were uprooted as the Venetians forced the islanders to cultivate olive trees, which adapted happily to the soil and climate and flourished throughout the island, to the extent that today they occupy about 30% of the land.

OLIVE CULTURE

Corfiots have been cultivating the olive for 5000 years, and there are said to be somewhere between three and four million olive trees on Corfu today. Harvesting is carried out in a most unusual way. The Corfiot growers do not pick the fruit or beat the branches with sticks, as is done elsewhere, but let the olives fall to the ground naturally. Neither do they prune their trees, with the result that they have some of the largest trees in Greece. It is quite usual in Greece for an olive tree to be owned by someone other than the owner of the land on which it grows, but the landowner must allow access to the tree.

The Venetians had a great impact on the look of the **buildings** as well as the countryside. Their influence can be seen everywhere in Corfu Town, with its many tall, balconied buildings, the shutters painted an Italian green rather than the usual bright blue of the Greek Aegean islands. Most churches, too, are in Venetian style, with separate bell towers and red-tiled roofs. The Venetians fortified the island, building Corfu Town's Old Fortress in 1550, followed by the New Fortress a mere 30 or so years later; gun batteries were everywhere.

Of less importance to Venice were the Corfiot working people. As long as they continued to produce the required olive oil, their education, emancipation and good health could be ignored. During the 17th century the arts flourished in the capital, while the people working the land suffered **plague** and **poverty**. In 1610 the Corfiot villagers had refused to pay rent to the landowners, forming armed vigilante bands to prevent Venetian troops from entering their villages to enforce the law. The dispute was settled diplomatically, but there were three more revolts in the 1640s and 1650s, accompanied by much violence, as the Venetian army attempted to put down the rebellions. Meanwhile, the aristocracy on Corfu had published its *Libro d'Oro* ('Golden Book'), which listed the most noble families, as did a similar book in Venice itself: Corfu and the Venetian empire were both in decline and the French in ascendancy.

Below: *The Liston, designed by Frenchman Mathieu de Lesseps, was built in 1807.*

The French in Corfu

Napoleon Bonaparte's General Gentili captured Corfu in 1797, and the French forces were greeted as liberators. They burned the 'Golden Book' in the main square and planted a Tree of Liberty on the site of the fire. With memories of the French Revolution (1789) still fresh in their minds, the Corfiots were delighted to have overthrown the Venetian ruling class.

Less delighted at the prospect of French rule in the Ionian Islands were the other great powers – Britain, Russia and, in particular, Turkey. In 1799 a joint Russian-Turkish venture took the island back from the French and declared the Ionian Islands a **'Septinsular Republic'**, the first glimmerings of the eventual emergence of a separate Greek state – another source of great Corfiot pride. The republic proved short-lived, as Russia and Turkey were soon at war with each other, and in 1807 the French returned to Corfu for a brief but productive period of seven years. During this time, the Ionian Academy was founded and use of the Greek language was re-established to replace Italian; printing was introduced, as too were the potato and the tomato, important additions to the island's agriculture.

British Rule (1814–64)

When Napoleon abdicated in 1814, both Britain and Austria claimed Corfu. In 1815 a treaty was signed which declared that, while the Ionian Islands would form a free and independent state, they would come under the exclusive protection of Britain. This was another short but vital period in the development of the Ionian Islands, as both they and Greece moved towards total independence and ultimate unification.

Below: *The British Garrison Church of St George was built in typical Greek style, though it is far from typical of Corfiot architecture.*

OFFSHORE EVENTS

Corfu's mainland neighbour, the region of Epirus, has had its share of despotic rulers. However, the Despot of Epirus was welcomed by the Corfiots in 1214 when he took the island from the Venetians. The ensuing rule of the Despotate was a golden period, when Ortho-dox Christianity flourished and Corfu prospered. A less benign figure is that of Ali Pasha, the maverick Turkish provincial governor of Epirus who, in defiance of the Ottoman central authority, carved out his own Greek empire in the early years of the 19th century. He was supported by the first British High Commissioner of Corfu, Sir Thomas Maitland, who in 1817 ceded him the main-land port of Parga – whose inhabitants promptly emig-rated to Corfu. Ali Pasha's activities, in distracting the Ottomans, facilitated the Greek uprising of 1821.

Greek now became Corfu's official language and the Ionian Academy its first University. The road network was improved and an aqueduct built to bring fresh water to Corfu Town. The face of the capital changed, with many new buildings and monuments going up; most still stand today and, as for instance the Palace of St Michael and St George and the Maitland Rotunda, add to the elegance of the town.

Meanwhile, momentum was gathering in the move-ment towards unification with Greece, which in 1829 had formally gained its **independence** from the Ottoman Empire after four centuries of Turkish rule. Britain wanted to hold on to Corfu because of its useful position between the ports of Italy and those of the Eastern Mediterranean, but the Corfiot determination to be part of the new Greek state won out, and the last British Commissioner, Sir Henry Storks, was appointed in 1859. Five years later, on 21 May 1864, the British flag was replaced by the Greek flag, flying for the first time above the Old Fortress in Corfu Town.

One of Corfu's most prominent sons, **Ioannis Kapodistrias**, became the first President of modern Greece after his close involvement in the struggle for liberation; sadly he did not live to see Corfu's inde-pendence as he was assassinated in 1831. Another important Corfiot statesman was **George Theotokis**, who served as Greece's prime minister several times.

Modern Corfu

Corfu grew increasingly attractive to visitors from both the Greek mainland and abroad, and in the late 19th and early 20th centuries was becoming a fashionable and prosperous island. The Mon Repos estate and villa served as the summer residence for the Greek royal family, while Elizabeth of Austria was such a regular visitor to the island that she built her own palace, the Achillion which is now open to visitors (see page 105). After the assassi-nation of Elizabeth, the Achillion was eventually bought by the German Kaiser, Wilhelm II. You can see his 'throne', a favourite sunset-viewing spot near Pelekas, and his 'bridge', more of a jetty, built to provide him with easy access to the Achillion when he arrived by sea.

Corfu was officially neutral during World War I, although it was used as a naval base (*see* panel, this page). It was in 1923 that the island entered the world stage when it came under attack from the Italians in what became known as the Corfu Incident. Arguments over Greece's northern border with Albania – continuing to this day – were being thrashed out by a commission, when the Italian delegate was murdered. His killer was never discovered. Because this happened on Greek soil, Mussolini attacked Corfu, Greece's nearest point to Italy, and occupied the island. Through the intervention of the League of Nations the Italians were eventually persuaded to leave.

Italy reoccupied Corfu during World War II, followed by the Germans; the island was liberated in 1944 by the advancing Allied Army. Since then, there has been a long period of stability, with a steady increase in tourism bringing prosperity to the islanders.

SERBIAN TRAGEDY

During World War I Corfu declared its neutrality, but was seized for use as a naval base by the British, French and Italian allies in December 1915. After the defeat of Serbia by Austria in 1916, the Serbian government and its troops retreated to Corfu. Already ravaged by cholera, many more of the Serbians died there from injuries, further disease and overcrowded living conditions. Their graves can be found in a Serbian cemetery on Vido Island.

Opposite: *Ioannis Kapodistrias became modern Greece's first President in 1827; his statue now stands at the top of the street which bears his name, Kapodistriou.*
Left: *The Achillion Palace has been a royal home, casino, hospital and film set, and is now a museum.*

Greece in the 20th Century

Although Corfu itself has enjoyed a period of relative stability since unification with Greece, the country as a whole has had a turbulent 20th century.

An ignominious end to World War I saw Greece defeated in its attempts to continue hostilities and capture Turkey, and in 1923 there was an **exchange of religious populations** under the Treaty of Lausanne when 388,000 Muslim Turks left Greece and no less than 1,300,000 Christian Greeks came home from Turkey. This had a shattering effect on a poor country whose population was then less than five million.

During World War II, German troops conquered the Greek mainland and its islands . Almost 500,000 Greeks died of starvation when food was given to the occupying armies.

Liberation only plunged the country into a vicious **Civil War** which lasted until late 1949. Many Greeks migrated to the United States, Canada and Australia. In 1967 there was further turmoil when a group led by Army Colonels seized power from an increasingly left-wing government in a **military coup**. The Junta was to last for seven years, its downfall brought about by inept handling of the situation in Cyprus, which resulted in the Turkish invasion of the northern part of that island and a dispute which, decades later, is still unresolved.

In the first post-Junta democratic elections of November 1974, the New Democracy Party (the main right-wing political party) came to power, and shortly afterwards a referendum voted for the **abolition of the monarchy**. King Constantine – who had gone into exile after his support of the Colonels' Junta – was replaced by a president. The royal summer residence on Corfu, Mon Repos, is now open to the public.

Several new political parties were formed in the wake of the Colonels, among them the socialist PASOK party (Pan Hellenic Socialist Movement), which was voted into power in the 1981 general elections. It was in the same year that Greece joined the **European Community** (EC).

PASOK formed the Greek government until 1989, but lost overall control after revelations of financial scandals involving the embezzlement of some £120 million from the Bank of Crete by one of its directors; PASOK ministers, and possibly even Prime Minister Papandreou, were implicated.

In April 1990 the right-wing New Democracy Party came to power, but their austerity measures proved unpopular and PASOK was returned to government in 1993. They oversaw the country's entry to the euro currency zone on 1 January 2002, and the planning of the Olympic Games in Athens in 2004. In March 2004 the New Democracy Party returned to power.

Left: *The Greek Parliament building on Athens's Syntagma Square.*

GOVERNMENT AND ECONOMY

Corfu is governed from Athens as a part of Greece. The **Greek parliament**, or *Vouli*, is made up of 300 members elected locally for four years using a form of proportional representation. Parliament elects a President for a term of five years and he in his turn chooses the Prime Minister, who heads the Council of Ministers, which is answerable to Parliament.

In addition, Corfu has a **Prefect** to represent its interests, a post which until recently was a political appointment by the government. In 1994 a move towards decentralization of the government gave the citizens of Corfu a chance to elect their own Prefect. They returned the PASOK-supporting Andreas Pagratis, who stood as a 'United Corfiot Movement' candidate and managed to receive over 32,000 votes – the support of 52% of the electorate.

The various regions of Corfu also have their own local, democratically elected politicians, headed by a **mayor**. In 1997 the borders of the municipality of Corfu, i.e. Corfu Town, were enlarged to include districts as far away as Gouvia and Kondokali, a move which caused much discussion in the local cafés. This municipality is the largest on the island, with about 40,000 inhabitants.

Economy

At the height of the tourist boom some eight million tourists visited Greece, accounting for some $2 billion – 7% of its GNP. Corfu received about 900,000 of these visitors, worth up to $250 million to the island's economy. About one-third of the working population is employed in **tourism** or ancillary service industries, such as construction, food and drink processing plants and the making of leather and other goods predominantly sold as souvenirs. A fall in tourist numbers has meant a rethink where Greece is trying to encourage quality tourism rather than package and backpacker tourism. Despite the importance of the tourist industry since the 1950s, Corfu is still very largely an **agricultural island:** 60% of its population works on the land, and 60% of the island is cultivated. Half of the cultivated land is given over to olive trees, an estimated 3.5 million of them. Evidence of fishing may be widely apparent – boats bobbing on the sea or fishermen sitting mending their nets in the coastal villages – but fishing is now more a tradition than an industry.

After olive trees and tourists, Corfu is notable for its healthy **wine industry**. Many island specialities are not available elsewhere in Greece, so visitors should take the chance to sample these. Corfu's kumquat liqueur is unique to the island. Other **fruits** – oranges, lemons, pears, peaches, apricots, apples, cherries and melons – are grown, while one of the delights of walking on the island is the opportunity to pick wild figs, straight from the branch. Also harvested are the nuts from the carob tree, as well as almonds and walnuts. The principal **vegetables** to find their way on to the restaurant plate are potatoes, tomatoes, cucumbers, beans, onions and aubergines.

TOURISM MATTERS

While it is a common belief that tourism has ruined Corfu (usually expressed by people who have never been there), it is more likely that the tourist industry has been the making of the island. In addition to direct employment in the service industries, farmers benefit from an increased demand for their produce, and jobs are created in the construction of hotels and other tourist facilities. If Corfu had not possessed international-standard facilities, the island would scarcely have been invited to host the 1994 European Union Summit – which further raised its profile.

Opposite: *Tourism is modern Greece's second largest money-earner.*
Below: *Corfu is well watered, and many rural families keep at least a few animals.*

GREEK ALPHABET

The Greek alphabet may look daunting at first, but it only takes an hour or so to memorize it. A knowledge of the alphabet will enable you to read road and other signs, and the destinations of local buses. The chart below shows upper and lower case characters of the alphabet, together with a guide to the pronunciation of their Greek names.

A	α	**ahl**fah
B	β	**vee**tah
Γ	γ	**ghah**mah
Δ	δ	**dhehl**tah
E	ε	**eh**pseelonn
Z	ζ	**zee**tah
H	η	**ee**tah
Θ	θ	**thee**tah
I	ι	**yee**otah
K	κ	**kah**pah
Λ	λ	**lahm**dhah
M	μ	mee
N	ν	nee
Ξ	ξ	ksee
O	o	**o**meekron
Π	π	pee
P	ρ	ro
Σ	σ	**seegh**mah
T	τ	tahf
Y	υ	**eep**seelonn
Φ	φ	fee
X	χ	khee
Ψ	ψ	psee
Ω	ω	om**eh**ghah

Right: *Handmade needle-lace is made all over Greece and is a popular souvenir. The lace is made by local women, often sitting on their doorsteps, chatting to fellow lacemakers and displaying their skills.*

THE PEOPLE

Although Corfu and the other Ionian islands have been a part of Greece for only 140 years, it is hard to imagine the Corfiot people being anything other than Greek. Of course there are the idiosyncratic British legacies of cricket, ginger beer and even Christmas pudding, but the Corfiot heart belongs to Greece. The language, the cooking and, most of all, the religion are Greek through and through.

Language

The official language is Greek, but in the tourist areas and capital you will find many speakers of English and other European languages, mainly German and Italian. Most information that the visitor is likely to need, such as on menus or notices and in museums, will be in both Greek and English, but this is not the case in the more rural areas. Similarly, while major road signs are in Greek and English, should you venture on to the minor roads – or wish to travel by bus round the island – it is useful to have a knowledge of the Greek alphabet.

Religion

As in other parts of Greece, the population of Corfu is almost 100% **Greek Orthodox**. There is a small **Catholic** community, whose services are held in the Roman Catholic Cathedral in the Town Hall Square in Corfu Town, while the British left behind a tiny **Anglican** congregation, who worship in the church of the Holy Trinity on Mavili. There is also a very small **Jewish** population. Before World War II there were 4,000 Jews on Corfu, all of whom were removed by the Germans; only 80 returned.

Above: *A resident monk outside the chapel of the monastery in Paleokastritsa.*

The Greek Orthodox church plays a central role in Corfiot lives. The closeness of the church to everyday family life is evident in the role of the priest, a familiar figure seen not just in and around the church but in the streets, in the shops and sitting in the cafés, talking with the men of his flock over a cup of coffee. While treated with great respect, a priest is a man like other men to the Greeks. Ordinary priests may marry, although marriage prevents a priest rising beyond a certain level in the Orthodox church.

Greek Orthodox church services are informal affairs – almost as much social as religious occasions. Because they are long (up to three hours), worshippers may attend for a short while, wander away and perhaps return later on. Foreign visitors (suitably attired) are welcome to enter the church during a service. At any one time during a normal weekly service, the congregation might appear quite small, centered on a hard core of ubiquitous old ladies dressed in black, but on major feasts such as Easter or the festival of St Spiridhon (Corfu's patron saint), it becomes apparent just how many of the population still follow the faith.

WORRY BEADS

In a traditional Corfiot café, where the men gather to discuss everything from politics to the price of fish, you will see many of them playing with a small set of beads in one hand. These are known as worry beads, though the name seems rather a contradiction in a nation whose national slogan ought to be 'no problem'. In fact the beads are used more out of habit while relaxing than as a means of relieving tension. They are popular souvenirs, being typically Greek, and are available in all sizes, all materials and all colours in most souvenir shops. The Greek word for them is **Komboloi**.

Right: *Religious festivals play a big part in Corfu life, and visitors shouldn't miss an opportunity to witness one of these events.*

Opposite: *Almost 1700 years after his death, the remains of St Spiridhon are still intact and enshrined in the church dedicated to him.*

Festivals

Saints' days, Carnival and, above all, Easter are reasons for Corfiots to come out on the streets of towns and villages to celebrate. If your visit to a particular village coincides with the local saint's day, you can hardly fail to be caught up in the general atmosphere of excitement as the saint's image is taken from his church and paraded through the streets in a lively procession. Afterwards there will be feasting and dancing, which you may well be invited to join.

Easter

Most impressive of all is Easter, the principal festival of the Orthodox year. Corfu has its own spectacular way of observing the feast, making this a good time to visit Corfu Town, though the weather can be uncertain and the evenings will be cool. Solemn processions take place on Good Friday, a sombre day of mourning. Then on Easter Saturday morning St Spiridhon is carried through the streets in a brilliant procession. What follows is unique to Corfu Town. At 11:00 the streets are emptied and mayhem breaks out, as unwanted crockery is hurled from every window on to the streets below. Nobody knows the origin of this extraordinary custom.

GETTING LOST

It is very easy to get lost driving around the island, or walking the maze of streets in Corfu Town. The Greek people like to be helpful and are likely to give you directions even if they don't know them. The general rule is to ask three people.

Evening mass climaxes at midnight, when the priest announces that Christ is risen. Electric lights are switched off and the priest ignites a solitary candle, from which the worshippers then light their own candles. Immediately church bells ring out, and fireworks blaze as the people make their way home for the Easter feast. In Corfu Town, the announcement of Christ's Resurrection is made from the bandstand on the Esplanade and is followed by church bells, music from the town bands and fireworks. Easter Sunday is a day for family celebrations, centred on a meal of roast lamb. There is often a communal evening celebration, at which visitors are welcome.

Other Festivals

Carnival is celebrated in Corfu Town on the last Sunday before Lent. After a colourful procession of floats accompanied by the town bands, an effigy representing the spirit of Carnival is ritually burnt.

'**Clean Monday**', the first day of Lent, is celebrated with a picnic (weather permitting) of seafood, salad, olives, special unleavened bread and halva, a honeyed sweet containing nuts and sesame seeds.

Corfu's patron saint, **St Spiridhon**, is the focus of several festivals. His remains are paraded in four annual processions (*see panel, page 39*) and his name day, 12 December, is shared by about half the male population of the island. On this day, the saint's body in its silver coffin is stood upright for the faithful to kiss his velvet slipper.

NAME DAYS

The Greeks celebrate not their birthday but their name day – the feast day of the saint after which they are named. So, every Maria or every Mikalis in one area will get together to celebrate in some way. This frequently means a big party. If you happen upon such an event, you will be made very welcome, although a small charge may be made to cover the cost of food and drink. Dancing and music frequently follow the meal.

SEAFOOD

Seafood can hardly be fresher than caught and served on the same day, but frozen fish is also served up and labelled as fresh in some tourist tavernas, so don't always believe what you're told. But if it's really fresh, the fish will be delicious. It will probably be expensive too, as fish stocks are low and prices high. Fish is priced by weight, so choose which piece you want rather than leaving it to the waiter – otherwise you could find yourself with an unexpectedly steep bill at the end of the meal.

Below: *Stuffed peppers are popular and tasty, but best eaten at lunch time when they are hot. Food is generally eaten lukewarm in the evenings. Greeks consider this better for the digestion.*

Food and Drink

Corfiot cuisine is, for the most part, identical to that available anywhere else in Greece, but it does have two specialities which appear on almost every restaurant menu. *Sofrito* is a veal casserole served with a white sauce of garlic, onion, pepper, wine vinegar and anything else the chef puts in to produce his version of the dish. Some serve a beef *sofrito*, though strictly speaking it is a veal dish. So too is *pastitsáda*, another island speciality – veal served in a tomato sauce with pasta. However, the veal might be beef, the pasta might be any kind and the sauce depends on the whim of the chef, so try it in different restaurants. Less common, but well worth eating if you come across it, is *bourdéto*, a casserole of white fish, onions, olive oil and spicy red peppers.

Another feature of dining on Corfu is its international flavour. The vast numbers of tourists have created a range of restaurants to cater for them, including Italian, Chinese, British, French and Indian. Most of the chefs are Greek or British, and as adept at producing a chicken vindaloo as a plate of roast beef and Yorkshire pudding.

There are several types of Greek eating establishments. Best known is the **taverna**, a casual place where it is usual for the diner to wander into the kitchen to see what's cooking, rather than to order from the menu: not all the menu's dishes are necessarily available, while the kitchen might conceal some daily specials. Another feature is the paper or plastic tablecloths which are changed after each meal, and the little tumblers which serve as wine glasses. If all the tables are occupied when you arrive, simply wait: another table will probably be produced from somewhere and set out for you. Greek tavernas are surprisingly expandable.

A **restaurant** (*estiatório*) is more up-market: you should find a proper wine-glass on the table, a linen tablecloth – and a surprised expression if you try to wander into the kitchen. Restaurants are more likely to take bookings, whereas at a taverna you generally turn up and take pot luck. For that reason, not all the recommended eating places in this guide have telephone numbers listed. Those with numbers take bookings, the others don't. In addition to regular tavernas and restaurants, there are places serving only fish (*psária*), and grill bars (*psistariés*), where the menu is generally limited to freshly grilled meats – chops or kebabs – and sometimes fish.

Above: *Greek wine wins no prizes, but apéritifs, spirits and liqueurs are plentiful and good value, with kumquat liqueur unique to Corfu.*

Greece is not noted for its puddings. A restaurant may have a small dessert menu, but in a taverna the only choice is likely to be fresh fruit (usually watermelon) or ice cream. It is common practice to eat your final course elsewhere, at a café which serves coffee, brandy and sticky Greek sweets such as **baklavá**.

The Greeks, generally, are not great drinkers and are likely to accompany a meal with no more than a can of beer or a soft drink. The pre-dinner favourite drink is **ouzo**, an aniseed-based drink similar to Pernod, which is served with a tumbler of water. You can drink the ouzo neat, taking an occasional sip of water, or you can dilute it by pouring water into the glass, which turns the ouzo milky. No Greek male would ever dilute his ouzo.

The cheapest wine available is **retsina**, an acquired taste – which many visitors never acquire. The white wine is flavoured with resin, originally from the wooden casks in which it was stored, but today the flavour is more likely to be added artificially. Not only is retsina cheap and available everywhere, it is in fact a good accompaniment to the oil-rich Greek food. Many tavernas serve it from the barrel, and a request for house wine will produce a metal jug of retsina. In it you have the authentic taste of Greece.

CHEERS!

The Greek equivalent of cheers when raising a glass is *yammas*, and the custom is to chink the glass of everyone else at the table. This can take some time, especially as the Greeks like to do it whenever their glasses are refilled. Make sure you always touch the top of your neighbour's glass with the top of your glass – to use the bottom is wishing a curse on the other person. Another drinking custom is the refilling of glasses whenever they are less than about half full. To drain a glass looks like greed, and to allow a glass to be empty is a slur on the host's hospitality.

2
Corfu Town

Corfu Town (Kerkyra to the locals) is as charming a capital as any in the Greek islands. With a population of almost 40,000 it is small enough to have retained its human scale, yet large enough to be cosmopolitan. This international feel is due partly to its location – it is closer to Italy than to Athens – and partly to its multicultural history.

The British presence may have lasted only 50 years, but it left a legacy unique in Greece, the game of cricket being just one eccentric part of this. On the grand scale, the villa of **Mon Repos** and the **Palace of St Michael and St George** were both built by the British. But the overall architectural appeal of the town is largely due to the Venetian influence, from the **Old** and **New Fortresses**, solid defences against onslaught from the sea, to the shuttered windows and narrow alleys. It was the French who first planted trees around the **Esplanade**, the grassy park at the heart of Corfu Town, and who were responsible for the **Liston**, the elegant terrace of cafés that borders the Esplanade, with its nod towards the Rue de Rivoli in Paris.

For all this, Corfu Town is undeniably Greek. Visit the Orthodox Cathedral or the church of the island's patron saint, St Spiridhon; explore the **Byzantine and Archaeological Museums**; eat in the tavernas, drink in the cafés of the Liston, visit the market near the New Fortress or watch the sun go down over the islets of **Vlacherna** and **Pontikonissi** (Mouse Island), and you could be nowhere else in the world but Greece.

Don't Miss

*** A visit to **Kanoni** and **Mouse Island**.
*** Sitting in the **Liston** with a coffee.
*** A stroll round the **Old Town**'s narrow streets.
*** The **Museum of Asiatic Art**'s unique collection.
** **Paper Money Museum** – unexpectedly fascinating.
** **Andivouniotissa Museum** of Byzantine artefacts.
** **Church of St Spiridhon**.
** The **Old Fortress** with stunning views.
** The imposing Gorgon Frieze in the **Archaeological Museum**.

Opposite: *The Liston, a touch of Parisian chic.*

Old and New Ports ★

Corfu Town has two ports, both on the northern side of town. The **New Port** (Nea Limani), in the suburb of Mandouki, is used mainly for international ferry routes, along with some boats to other Greek islands and the mainland. From here it is a walkable distance into the town centre, or you can take a taxi from the rank outside; there is no bus service.

The smaller daily ferries to Igoumenitsa on the mainland and to the island of Paxos depart from the **Old Port** (Paleo Limani), to the east of the New Fortress. Tickets for trips can be bought from any of the several ticket offices both behind and to the east of the port itself, on Athinagora and Donzelot streets. The Old Port is a low-key affair: as small fishing boats moored in the harbour rock gently on the water, you can imagine what Corfu Town might have been like in the old days, before the island became a magnet for tourism.

Greater Corfu

New Fortress ★

The New Fortress, or Neo Frourio ('new' because it was built some 30 years after the Old Fortress) dominates the Old Port. The Venetians started building it in 1576, and completed it 13 years later; the British added the buildings at the very top in 1815. The view from here – of Corfu Town, surrounding villages, Mount Pantokrator to the north and across to mainland Greece and Albania – is excellent. For a long time the Fortress was used as a training establishment for the Greek Navy and was closed to the public but today for a small fee you can explore its dungeons, tunnels and battlements, and enjoy a drink in the café at the top. There is also a small **gallery** and a **ceramics museum**. Down below is the lively fruit and vegetable **market** held daily in what was the moat. This can be reached through a small tunnel lying above and behind New Fortress Square.

Old Town ★★★

The well used phrase 'a maze of streets' takes on fresh significance when you start to meander through the **narrow streets** and even narrower alleyways that cluster higgledy-piggledy between the Old and New Forts, in the northern half of Corfu Town.

It would surely take a lifetime fully to know your way around; new arrivals should simply try their best to keep some sense of direction – though the fun is in getting slightly lost and exploring what look like interesting side streets.

Thirty years ago you might have seen donkeys clopping down some of these tiny passageways, their loads brushing against both walls, but now scooters buzz noisily through. Washing frequently hangs drying above your head, suspended across the wider streets, and you might see a housewife lowering a basket from her balcony to buy goods from a tradesman in the street below. There are tourist shops, bakeries, bars and other establishments all hidden away in the whitewashed alleys – so explore, but take care not to get totally lost.

The official **National Tourist Office of Greece** in Corfu Town has been closed for a few years but a new one was due to open opposite the Town Hall at the time of writing.

Above: *The Old Port has domestic ferries and other craft; international services depart from the New Port.*

UNDERNEATH THE ARCADES

The attractive arcaded streets of Corfu Town are not merely of architectural interest, but also reflect the varied climate of this island. They provide protection from the hot sun of summer and from the heavy rains of winter. They shelter the coffee-drinkers and newspaper-readers whiling away the hours on the Liston, the tourists looking for postcards and souvenirs in the Old Town, and the local shoppers stocking up at bakers' and grocers' shops in the back streets.

Andivouniotissa Museum ★★

At the top of a flight of steps off Arsinou, and marked by a signpost, is an impressive **Byzantine** Museum. The small but very varied collection is well displayed in the Church of Panayia Andivouniotissa. Probably built in the late 15th century, the church was privately owned until 1979, when it was handed over to the Greek state on condition that it be turned into a museum. After repair work was carried out, the doors were first opened in 1984 by Melina Mercouri, the well-known actress who was then Greek Minister of Culture. By 1994 the final stage of restoration was completed, and a fuller new collection of icons put on display, many from the church itself. There are also old wall paintings.

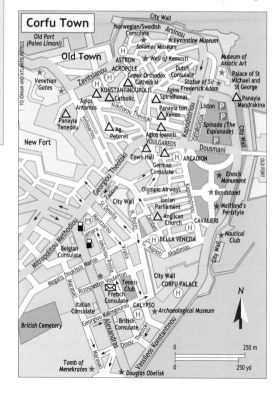

The collection of about 90 **icons** ranges in date from the 15th to the 19th centuries, most being from the 17th and 18th centuries. They include the usual goodly number of portraits of the saints, but it is the wide range of Biblical scenes, such as the *Stoning of St Stephen* and the *Washing of the Feet of Jesus*, that makes the collection particularly interesting. Most of the icons are as vividly colourful as the day they were painted. Around the walls of the church hang several very fine 'Scenes from the Old Testament' by the 17th- to 18th-century artist, Konstandinos Kontarines.

POET OF THE PEOPLE

Although he was born on Zakynthos in 1798, the poet **Dionysios Solomos** moved to Corfu in 1828 and stayed there until his death in 1857. He was at the heart of the intellectual revival on Corfu, and was especially popular as the first poet to use the ordinary spoken Greek for his work, not classical Greek as all writers before him had used. He believed that literature should be available for everyone to read, not just an elite. Every Greek now knows his work, for part of his poem *Hymn to Freedom* was set to music to become the Greek national anthem.

Left: *Enter the newly refurbished Byzantine Museum to admire Corfiot icons, paintings and carvings.*

CORFU LITERARY SOCIETY

To the left of the Palace of St Michael and St George is a graceful building with an outside staircase leading to the Corfu Literary Society. Founded in 1836, the society claimed most of Corfu's leading intellectual figures as members. Though not generally open to the public, it frequently mounts exhibitions and its collection of some 10,000 volumes about the Ionian Islands can be consulted by genuine scholars. It also houses collections of maps, engravings, paintings, photographs and newspapers, and produces its own publications.

Also important is the Cretan connection. During its period of Venetian rule from the 13th to the 17th centuries, Crete was Greece's most important artistic centre. As Corfu was a stopping-point on the route from Crete to Venice, many of the most talented artists from the Cretan School both visited and lived on the island for short periods. Some of their works survived and are on display here, as is explained in the informative notes (in Greek and English) on the museum's walls.

Solomos Museum ★

Also signposted just off Arsinou and close to the Andivouniotissa Museum is the house where the Ionian poet, **Dionysios Solomos** lived until his death in 1857. Open Monday–Saturday mornings, it will be of interest mainly to enthusiasts and those with a good knowledge of the Greek language – very little information is given in anything other than Greek. There are old photographs and oil paintings of the poet, an original manuscript, the desk at which he wrote and other memorabilia, as well as the chance to see inside his former home, but this museum is not likely to detain the average visitor for long.

Palace of St Michael and St George ★

The Order of St Michael and St George was created in 1818, the year before the five-year construction of this palace began, to honour British civil servants who had served with distinction in Malta and the Ionian Islands. The palace, built as a base for the Order and a residence for the British High Commissioner, is constructed from Maltese limestone. It stands at the northern edge of the Esplanade, fronted by a statue of **Sir Frederick Adam**, the British High Commissioner who pioneered the popularity of Paleokastritsa and built the Mon Repos villa to the south of Corfu Town.

In 1864, when the British left, the palace became a residence for the Greek royal family but later fell into ruin. It was restored in the 1950s by the British Ambassador to Greece, Sir Charles Peake, who was keen to see the palace renovated and used in view of its British connections.

GREEK POETIC TRADITION

Greece has a fine poetic tradition, with the rare distinction of two of its poets having won the Nobel Prize for Literature, an honour indeed for what is a minority language. **Odysseus Elytis** won the prize in 1979, while George Seferis had been given the award in 1963. It was yet another Nobel Prizewinner, Rudyard Kipling, who first translated Dionysios Solomos's 'Hymn to Freedom' into English.

The west wing is now home to both the Tourist and Traffic Police, the eastern end of the building contains archive offices and a public library, and the splendid former State Rooms house the Museum of Asiatic Art (*see* below). The Palace is also home to the small **Municipal Art Gallery**, which has some changing exhibitions and is worth checking out.

Museum of Asiatic Art ★★

The grandly restored State Rooms of the Palace of St Michael and St George house a collection of Asiatic art considered one of the finest in the world. The core of the museum, containing items from China, Japan, Tibet, Nepal and other Asian nations, was originally amassed by the Corfiot diplomat **Gregorios Manos**. His 10,000-piece collection was given to the state in 1927, and later bequests – from a Greek Ambassador to India, Japan and Korea and a Greek merchant based in the Netherlands – extended the scope of the collection. The result is a splendid and varied display, ranging from Buddhas to bronzes, from stonework to silk, and from armour to delicate porcelain as well as erotic Indian woodcarvings.

Above: *The Palace of St Michael and St George houses government departments, police offices and a museum.*

COLLECTOR EXTRAORDINARY

A passionate collector of oriental art, **Gregorios Manos** was born on Corfu and rose to become a diplomat. In 1919, when he was Greek Ambassador to Austria, he offered his large collection to the state, on the condition that he could retire on a pension and spend the rest of his life as curator of the Museum of Sino-Japanese Art (as it then would have been called). Agreement was not reached until 1927, and sadly the following year Manos died in poverty, all his wealth having gone into his beloved art collection.

Cathedral ★

Corfu's Orthodox Cathedral stands impressively at the top of a wide flight of steps near the Old Port. Built in 1577, it has been a cathedral only since 1841 and is known as the Cathedral of the Panayia Spiliotissa (Madonna of the Cave), or by the more familiar name of Mitropolis (Cathedral). In fact it is dedicated to **St Theodora**, whose remains were brought to the island from Constantinople at the same time as those of St Spiridhon; her preserved body is kept in a silver coffin to the right of the altar. Theodora was a Byzantine Empress, revered for reinstating the worship of icons; like St Spiridhon, her only connection with Corfu is the presence here of her body, worshipped once a year when her coffin is opened. The Cathedral has the usual array of icons, the most notable being one of St George just inside the door. The interior is gloomily impressive, the three aisles making it broader and squatter than many Orthodox churches, but it cannot be described as either beautiful or of significant historical interest.

Right: *It is illegal to export genuine antique icons, but modern reproductions are of a very high standard and are an undeniably Greek memento.*

Left: *Separate bell towers, as here at the Church of St Spiridhon, are unusual in Greece but are a common feature on Corfu due to Italian influences.*

Church of St Spiridhon ★★

At the end of the street named Spiridonos is the **holiest place on Corfu**. Here stands the church of St Spiridhon, its red-domed belfry the tallest on the island and a landmark as you head into the town from the Esplanade. The church was built in 1589 and dedicated to the saint whose mummified body it was intended to house. Spiridhon's remains had been wrapped in a sack of straw, tied to the back of a donkey and smuggled out of Constantinople in 1460 when the Turkish occupation was imminent.

Brought up as a shepherd on Cyprus, **Spiridhon** became first a monk then a bishop, and many minor miracles had been credited to him before his death in 350. When his body was later exhumed it had not decayed, and the saint's holy powers were reinforced. Chance led his remains to be taken to Corfu, but he quickly became the island's patron saint and has been revered for the last 500 years. Oddly enough, St Spiridhon's body remained the property of the descendants of the priest who had originally smuggled him out of Constantinople, only being handed to the church in 1927. Four times a year the saint's body – otherwise kept in its silver coffin to the right of the altar – is carried around the town in a procession.

> **THANKS TO ST SPIRIDHON**
>
> There are four days a year when the mummified remains of St Spiridhon are taken from his church and carried in procession around Corfu Town. It is something not to be missed, if your visit coincides with Palm Sunday, Easter Saturday, 11 August or the first Sunday in November. Each procession commemorates a different occasion on which the revered saint came to the help of the island: he has averted two plagues, one famine and one Turkish invasion attempt.

Above: *The Earl of Guilford, one of Corfu's most colourful characters.*

THE EARL OF GUILFORD

One of the most un-Greek street names in Corfu Town is Guilford Street, named in honour of the fifth Earl of Guilford (1769–1828). He was a colourful British eccentric who lived on Corfu in the early 19th century, given to wearing golden wreaths and purple robes. He converted to the Greek Orthodox faith and reopened the Ionian Academy, which became the first university in modern Greece. Guilford is also remembered in a small park, named after him, just north of the entrance to the Old Fort. He sits there in stone, suitably robed.

Visitors to the church can sit and watch as a constant flow of visitors come to light candles and make their way to the coffin to kiss it and pray to St Spiridhon for help. Above the coffin hang dozens of silver thuribles (censers), while the church is crammed with silver candlesticks and votive offerings. The ceiling is decorated with some exquisite paintings.

Paper Money Museum ★★

Unlikely though it may seem, this is a fascinating museum. It is in Iroon Kypriakou Square, immediately south of the Church of St Spiridhon, housed above the **Ionian Bank** (constructed in 1846) in spacious rooms that were once the manager's residence.

The collection occupies several rooms, is open Monday–Saturday, 09:00–13:00 (free entry), and has information in Greek and English. The museum has a complete collection of **Greek bank notes** up to the present day, and through these you can follow the flow of Corfu's more recent history. British pounds give way to drachmas; notes in Italian and German come into use during World War II to be followed by British pounds again, for military use only; then comes wild inflation, with notes up to 400 billion drachmas.

Upstairs is perhaps the most interesting part of the museum, where several rooms tell the full story of the 'simple' **production of a bank note**: which paper to use, how watermarks and other anti-forgery devices are implemented, and the complex procedures involved in the design and printing processes. The intricate work demanded of an engraver is given its full due, and the evolution of the tricky business of numbering notes is explained, as is the question of security at the printing works. Money will never seem the same again after a visit to this museum, claimed to be the only one of its kind in the world.

Old Fortress (Paleo Frourio) ★★

A single passageway connects the outcrop on which the Old Fortress stands with the eastern end of the Esplanade. Although the present Venetian remains were built in 1550, it is believed that there have been fortifications on this promontory since the 7th or 8th century. Until 1979 the area was used by the Greek Army, who then handed it over to the Greek Archaeological Service to begin restoration work. Access to much of the site was restricted until recently, when a hefty admission fee was introduced for which visitors get little more than a splendid view over Corfu Town from the **Castel Nuovo lighthouse** at the very top. Beyond the rooftops of the town, the northeastern corner of the island can be clearly seen, with Mount Pantokrator standing supreme. Resorts such as Nissaki are plainly visible, while further to the right is the mainland of Albania and Greece. The southern suburbs of Corfu Town can be made out, with the airport runway and the magnificent southern sweep of the island off to the left.

The view apart, there is not much else here to detain the visitor for long. To the right of the entrance, situated around a corner, is a building which looks rather like the Parthenon's younger brother. This is the **Church of St George**, built by the British in 1840 for the use of the garrison which was then stationed here. It was badly bombed during World War II, then restored but later allowed to fall into further disrepair. It is now closed to visitors, a disharmonious eyesore.

There is also a small but interesting **Byzantine museum**, with some beautiful mosaics and frescoes. Admission is included in the cost of the ticket to the Fortress.

THE GREAT DEFENDER

Beside the entrance to the Old Fortress is the statue of Count John Matthias von der Schulenburg, whose most notable achievement on Corfu was to mastermind the defence against the attempted Turkish invasion of 1716. A Saxon mercenary in the pay of the ruling Venetian government, he was put in charge of the island's defence. On 8 August he led an army of the besieged from the Old Fortress in a surprise counter-attack which coincided with a violent storm (a helping hand from St Spiridhon perhaps). Three days later the Turks left the island.

Below: *Rock-solid for centuries, Corfu's Old Fortress is still being explored by archaeologists.*

The Esplanade ★★★

The open space directly in front of the Old Fortress, once used as a parade ground for both Venetian and British soldiers, is said to be the largest square in Greece. To the north of the Esplanade, as it is called, is the Palace of St Michael and St George, while its western border is formed by the arcaded street known as the **Liston**, a favourite place for Corfiots to see and be seen. Built by a Frenchman along the lines of the rue de Rivoli in Paris, the elegant Liston is a terrace of coffee shops, with a few restaurants and souvenir shops for good measure. Your cup of coffee will be pricier here than anywhere else in town, but you are paying for the buzz and bustle.

Surrounded by a number of palms, Judas trees and eucalyptuses, the Esplanade is a pleasant spot – even though it is one of the town's main parking areas. The northern half includes Corfu's famous **cricket pitch**, a somewhat less lethal use than the Venetians made of it – the area was a firing range. In the southern section there is a fountain, a **bandstand** regularly used for summer concerts, and a **rotunda**, built in 1816 in memory of the first British Lord High Commissioner to Corfu, Sir Thomas Maitland.

Directly across the main road from the rotunda is a statue to one of Corfu's most famous citizens, **Ioannis Kapodistrias**, who became the first president of modern Greece in 1827. He is buried in the Platytera Monastery (*see* page 46), and the **Kapodistrias Museum** has been created in his former home near the suburb of Evropouli.

The Town Hall ★

The Town Hall is one of Corfu Town's most appealing buildings, built by the Venetians as a single-storey assembly room in the late 17th century using **white marble** that was quarried near Mount

Below: *The Maitland Rotunda may appeal to the visitor, but ironically it stands opposite the statue of Ioannis Kapodistrias, who disliked Maitland and his British policies.*

Pantokrator. After use as a theatre and opera house, it eventually became the Town Hall in 1903 when the British added a second floor. In the attractive little square outside is good evidence of Corfu's diverse climate: on one side stands a palm tree, on the other a pine. Beyond are a fountain and café, and to one side is the Roman Catholic **Cathedral of St James**.

Archaeological Museum ★★

A few minutes' walk south of the town centre, along the sea front and just past the Corfu Palace hotel, you will find this very pleasing modern museum in Vraila, a side street to the right. Open daily from 08:30–15:00, except on Mondays; tel: 26610 30680.

As you climb the stairs to the first-floor rooms, be sure to look out for the **funerary stele** from the late 3rd or early 2nd century BC. It bears the inscription: 'You went 23 years old into the Underworld and left your mother Arpalis in mourning, your husband Aristandros widower and the children orphan. You chose for yourself the last sleep.' What family tragedy lies behind those enigmatic words?

Entering the central room you see at the far end a **carved crouching lion**, found near the Tomb of

Above: *Built during the French occupation, the Liston Arcade is popular with tourists and locals.*

FIND THE PRESIDENT

The museum dedicated to **Ioannis Kapodistrias**, Corfu's most famous political figure, is on the outskirts of Corfu Town and not easy to find. Ask for directions when you get to the suburb of Evropouli. Housed in the family residence, it contains a display of furniture, books and medals belonging to the great patriot who dedicated his early life to the cause of Greek independence and became Greece's first President. Kapodistrias was born into an aristocratic Corfiot family in 1776, and assassinated in Nafplion in the Peloponnese in 1831. The museum is open on Wed and Sat mornings only.

Above: *Corfu's Town Hall (on the left) was an opera house at one time.*

WINE, WOMEN ...

As well as the major highlights described, the **Archaeological Museum** contains many minor delights as well. Look for the small statue of Aphrodite, the Goddess of Love, herself clothed but leaning against a statuette of a woman lifting her dress to reveal her naked body. A pediment from about 500BC, found near Kanoni, shows a carving of a Dionysian feast, with Dionysos himself holding a drinking horn full of wine.

Menekrates in 1843, an important work from the 7th century BC. The wall behind this cleverly masks the entrance to the far room, which houses the museum's prime exhibit: **the Gorgon Pediment**. This makes a terrific impact as you turn the corner and see the huge frieze in all its terrifying glory, 17m (56ft) long and 3m (9ft) high with, at its centre, the grimacing figure of the Gorgon herself. Her waistband consists of two entwined, battling snakes and more serpents make up her hair. In fact the frieze is not consistent with the myth of the Gorgon: here she is is depicted flanked by her two offspring, Pegasus and Chrysaor, whereas mythology has it that her two children sprang from her blood when she was beheaded by Perseus. Little remains of the figure of Pegasus, though Chrysaor can be clearly seen holding a sword. The frieze is not intact, but the modern insertions to complete the impression do not detract from the most important archaeological find on Corfu, and one of the most powerful pieces of Greek sculpture outside the National Archaeological Museum in Athens. Dating from

590–580BC, it originally adorned the Temple of Artemis in ancient Kerkyra, sited at Paleopolis. Other finds from the temple are displayed around the same room.

Don't let the domineering Gorgon distract you from the many smaller gems on display here, such as a fine bronze of a naked warrior and some clay theatrical masks. The museum also contains a comprehensive collection of some 10,000 coins, as well as bronzes and clay statuettes, many of them from the excavations on the Mon Repos estate, to the south of Corfu Town. There are lead tablets dating from the 6th and 5th centuries BC, inscribed with acknowledgements of debts, while the earliest exhibits include Neolithic fragments dating back to the 6th millennium BC.

Tomb of Menekrates ★

Archaeology buffs will want to see this well preserved, roofed tomb of the 7th or 6th century BC – though it is unlikely to be the highlight of anyone's visit to Corfu. To find it, walk south along the sea front, past the Archaeological Museum, until you reach an obelisk at a junction of several roads. Go up Menekratous, which is to the left of the British Consulate building, until you come to the police station, whose grounds are the unlikely site of Menekrates' resting place: this area served as the cemetery of the ancient city of Kerkyra. The circular structure is built of roughly dressed stones and has a conical roof which, though probably a later replacement, is almost certainly similar in appearance to the tomb's original roof.

A Corfiot consul on the Greek mainland, **Menekrates** was evidently a popular, or at least an important figure. After he drowned at sea, he was commemorated by this elaborate memorial, discovered in 1843. Its interest to historians is the fact that it is intact, but casual visitors can see only the couple of metres of it that are visible above the present ground level. Fenced off behind green railings, the tomb looks neglected, overgrown as it is with moss and surrounded by empty drink cans, sweet wrappers and other litter.

PEGASUS

The winged horse, Pegasus, was the son of the union between Poseidon and Medusa, the Gorgon. Shortly after being born Pegasus pawed the ground on Mount Helicon, which caused a spring to flow and this spring was later believed to be the source for all poetic inspiration. Pegasus eventually joined the Gods on Mount Olympus, where it was his duty to bring Zeus his lightning and thunderbolts.

SIR HOWARD DOUGLAS

Major-General Sir Howard Douglas, Lord High Commissioner to the Ionian Islands from 1835 until 1840, was a military strategist and author of the first book on the subject of naval gunnery. During his term of office he improved the infrastructure of the islands and was the driving force behind the establishment of the Ionian Bank. An obelisk in his honour was erected in 1841 and stands on the coast road going south out of Corfu Town, just beyond the Corfu Palace Hotel and close to the Tomb of Menekrates.

British Cemetery ★★

From Platia Yioryiou Theotoki, more familiarly known as San Rocco Square, the British Cemetery is five minutes' walk along the airport road, Dimoulitsa. A small sign points you down a side street, past the mental hospital, into a green retreat. The door rings a bell as you enter, bringing out the caretaker, a kindly man who explains a little about the cemetery in broken English.

The secluded nature of the grounds is indicated by the fact that over 25 species of orchid have been found here, while goldcrests and great tits flutter and twitter in the pine trees. The cemetery began as a burial place for the British troops and other personnel who were stationed here, but has expanded to take in the British community generally, while one corner is given over to German graves. Nearby is an orchard of apple and orange trees, lovingly tended.

This is a moving as well as a peaceful place. Some graves are marked by simple wooden crosses – 'Harry Casson 1927–1983' – while other memorials tell tragic

stories of mothers and babies dying in childbirth. Young men lost in battle are remembered here, notably in the graves and memorial to 44 British sailors who lost their lives to Albanian mines while sailing in the Corfu channel in 1946, the incident that led to the severing of official British relations with Albania (*see* panel, page 69).

Monastery of Platytera ★

A former convent, but more frequently referred to as a monastery, this is open to the public, but no longer in use. To reach it, take a 10-minute walk down Polikhroniou Konstanda, off San Rocco Square. This is a pleasant arcaded street, appetisingly filled with butchers, bakers and patisseries, though the traffic heading out for Paleokastritsa can be very heavy. Where the road forks, take the right-hand option and you will see the monastery's red-topped bell tower ahead.

Enter the **courtyard** through a stone archway, between two palms – but heed the notice which says: 'You are kindly requested to enter this holy place properly dressed.' The well kept courtyard has bright white walls, green shutters and doors, a stone well and corners draped with bougainvillaea – an idyllic scene, though even here you don't quite escape the worst of the traffic noise.

It is more peaceful inside the church, but the dim light makes it difficult to appreciate the **fine icons** and paintings for which it is renowned, including several paintings by Koutouzis, a leading 18th-century artist, and some excellent ceiling paintings. The church was built in 1743, but virtually destroyed by French attacks on the island and rebuilt in 1801. Behind the ornate altarscreen, and not always accessible, is the surprisingly simple tomb of the great Corfiot hero, **Ioannis Kapodistrias**. If a priest is on duty and you express an interest in seeing the tomb, a small donation to the church's funds might secure you the privilege. Also buried here is Fotos Tzavellas, one of the leading figures in the Greek War of Independence.

Above: *Cool and quiet – the Monastery of Platytera.* **Opposite:** *The British Cemetery is well maintained thanks to the War Graves Commission, which pays for its upkeep.*

Church of St Jason and St Sosipater ★★

In the southern suburb of Anemomylos, this is the only complete and authentic **Byzantine church** on Corfu and probably dates back to the 11th century, though it may be even earlier. The building is superb, in brick and red tile, with a bell tower and octagonal dome. Inside the entrance are two icons of the saints to whom it is dedicated, Jason of Tarsus and Sosipater of Iconium. Both were bishops and disciples of St Paul, and they are believed to have brought Christianity to Corfu in the 1st century AD, probably during the reign of the notorious Roman Emperor Caligula. They later suffered the unusual martyrdom of being incarcerated in a bronze bull and burnt to death. The icons are believed to be the work of a 16th-century Cretan painter, Emanuel Tzanes, who also painted some of the other works around the walls. The very faded **wall paintings** also to be seen include an 11th-century fresco, just inside the entrance, showing a 10th-century Bishop of Corfu.

GLADSTONE IN CORFU

The great Victorian statesman William Gladstone (1809–98) visited the Ionian Islands in 1858, then under British rule, in order to discuss the dissatisfaction the islanders were feeling. There was at that time a great movement towards unification with mainland Greece, which had gained its own independence from the Turks in 1827. Gladstone became High Commissioner Extraordinary for a short period, but his proposals for reform were not accepted by the islanders and in 1863 formal moves were made for Britain to leave the Ionian Islands in favour of Greece.

Above: *The Church of St Jason and St Sosipater stands in the street which bears its name: Iassonios Sossipatriou.*

Mon Repos ★★

The area around the Mon Repos villa has an interesting history and the new museum of Palaiópolis. Less than an hour's walk south of Corfu Town along the sea road, this was the centre of the ancient city of Kerkyra, and several of the old city's remains are visible but not visitable.

The 5th-century BC historian Thucydides, in his account of the civil war on Corfu, which broke out while the island's military forces were engaged in the Peloponnesian War (*see* page 12), refers to the city of Kerkyra. Through him we know of the *agora* (market place), two harbours and three temples that existed then. The city spread over the greater part of the peninsula between the southern section of Garitsa Bay, which had the Harbour of Alkinoos, and Halikiopoulos Lagoon, with the Hyllaic Harbour. The northern extent of the ancient city can be seen in a fragment of its fortification wall preserved near the modern cemetery (it survived through being incorporated in a church).

The first thing you come to is the entrance to the Mon Repos beach, though access is restricted to the beach, bar and restaurant at this corner of the estate. The beach is not wonderful, but is packed at the height of summer, especially at weekends.

A short distance past the entrance to the beach are some of the remains of the **old city**, known as Paleopolis (literally, 'old city'). On the right is **Agia Kerkyra**, the city's church, an impressive ruin whose surviving walls, despite repeated destruction and rebuilding of the church, date back to the 5th century. It was built by Jovian, Bishop of Corfu, on the site of a pagan temple, which has been dated to the 5th century BC. The body of the church was destroyed in the 6th century, rebuilt, destroyed again in the 11th century, rebuilt, fell into disrepair, was renovated in 1537 and finally destroyed again in the bombings of World War II. In 1968, all the early Christian architectural parts, parapets, capitals etc., were collected and stored in the Old Palace Museum. The church's mosaics were restored in 1960 and 1969.

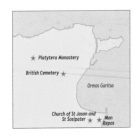

Below: *This view from the Old Fortress shows how the modern town grew up near here for defence purposes, while the old city has since crumbled.*

THE GORGONS

The best known characteristic of the Gorgons of Greek mythology is that with one glance they could turn a victim to stone. There were three Gorgons, the daughters of the sea god Phorcys and his wife, Ceto. These attractive creatures had teeth like tusks, snakes for hair, protruding tongues, wings, ugly faces and golden scales. Of the three, Medusa is the only one not immortal, which means that her sisters, Stheno and Euryale, must still be around somewhere.

The road beside the church leads down to the few remains of the **Temple of Artemis**, from which came the Gorgon Frieze in the Archaeological Museum. You need to exercise your imagination to make sense of the various fragments of the old city which have been excavated. There are some remnants of the city walls, as well as part of the aqueduct and the old port – now well inland.

Opposite the Church of Agia Kerkyra are the walled entrance gates to the **Mon Repos villa**. This was built in 1824 by the British High Commissioner, Sir Frederick Adam, as a present for his wife. When the British left Corfu it fell into the hands of the Greek royal family, one of whose descendants was born there and was later to marry into the British royal family (*see* panel, opposite).

The villa and grounds are now open to the public (grounds daily, 08:00–19:30; villa daily, 08:30–19:30)

Right: *Fifth-century ruins of Agia Kerkyra, the church of the old city.*

Left: *Statue of Sir Frederick Adam, the man responsible for the Mon Repos villa, which he built on the site of a pavilion which had been erected there by a Russian general.*

and the villa houses the excellent Museum of Palaiópolis, which tells the history of the house and the area. The grounds are beautifully wooded, making it a pleasant place for a stroll.

Also opposite Agia Kerkyra is the site of Roman Baths, still being excavated. The road between the baths and the church leads up to the village of Analipsis. **Analipsis** means 'Ascension', and a good day to visit is the Feast of the Ascension, 40 days after Easter Sunday, when the whole of the village and seemingly half of Corfu Town turns out to celebrate the occasion. In the village is a path by the Taverna Kardaki which passes a spring gushing from the mouth of a Venetian stone lion's head in the rock face. This is the well-known **Kardaki water**, one sip of which – according to the inscription – will ensure that you completely forget your homeland.

Also in Analipsis are the remains of the **Temple of Kardaki**. This temple was discovered when the spring stopped flowing in 1822, and the British Colonel in charge set his men digging to find the cause of the blockage. It

FROM CORFU TO EDINBURGH

Prince Philip, husband of Britain's Queen Elizabeth II, was born in the villa of Mon Repos on 10 June 1921. His father was Prince Andrew of Greece, who was a great-great-grandson of Queen Victoria. Prince Philip grew up in England and married Princess Elizabeth in 1947, when he became the Duke of Edinburgh. In 1957 he was made a Prince of the United Kingdom.

OLD STONES

Corfu is not particularly fruitful for archaeology and history buffs, as few reasonable remains have survived and there is still much exploration to be done. The best sites are:
• The remnants of **Paleopolis**, near Analipsis between Corfu Town and Kanoni
• **Angelokastro**, ruins of an impressive 13th-century fortress near Paleokastritsa
• **Gardiki**, southern Corfu, site of a Palaeolithic settlement (no traces visible), and neglected ruins of a 13th-century fortress.

was found that the hidden temple's altar had slipped in the ground, diverting the flow of the stream; the temple was excavated to restore the spring. Probably dedicated to Apollo, this small temple was built late in the 6th century BC and is the best preserved in the whole of Corfu. It had 11 columns along each side and six at the two ends. You can reach the temple by taking the left fork where the main road divides into the one-way system, then taking the first left, leading uphill.

Further remains of the ancient city are hidden away in the Mon Repos estate, including the ruins of Corfu's largest temple, which was probably dedicated to Hera and is known to have been reconstructed in the 4th century BC.

Right: *At the busiest spot on Corfu, Pontikonissi, the humble Greek fishing boat still bobs in the waters.*

Kanoni ★★★

The two narrow roads through Analipsis to Kanoni, at the end of the peninsula south of Corfu Town, have been turned into a one-way system. The low road takes drivers past the smaller properties of this residential area, while the high road returns them through the more select part of Kanoni, where the Corfu Holiday Palace hotel (previously the Corfu Hilton) is located.

Kanoni was once a pleasant retreat, a favoured picnic spot. Today it is a select address for Corfiot residents and also the hub of a separate tourist development, poised between Corfu Town and the next coastal resorts to the south, Perama and Benitses. There are several hotels, apartment blocks, restaurants, souvenir shops and cafés, and it would be a good base for a holiday, with easy access to Corfu Town and the eastern coast, if it were not for one considerable drawback – it is under the **airport** flight path. Watching planes come and go while sitting over a cup of coffee is pleasant enough for an hour or so; whether you would want to endure it for two weeks is another matter.

The daily assault on the ears from the aeroplanes bringing invading holiday-makers is appropriate, as Kanoni means 'battery'. The name comes from the days when the French installed an artillery battery here in 1798, and a large cannon from that time remains in the little square surrounded by shops and cafés, one of which offers an unrivalled view of the most photographed sight in Corfu, if not Greece – the islands of Pontikonissi and Vlacherna out in the bay. The cafés' prices are tailored accordingly.

A regular bus service runs from Corfu Town to the tip of the Kanoni peninsula, but if you enjoy walking it is not more than a stroll of an hour or so into the centre of Corfu Town. Certainly the British who used to favour this spot during their 50-year rule on Corfu would walk out to it in the evenings just as the Greeks today enjoy their Volta. However, the writer and artist Edward Lear complained on one of his visits to the island and refused to go 'pottering to the one-gun battery'.

PROGRESS?

Kanoni is typical of the way Corfu has changed over the years, particularly since the 1950s when the number of visitors started to increase. Many quiet fishing villages have gone, to be replaced by rows of hotels, villas, tavernas, bars, discos and tourist shops. That is not to say that these changes should only be lamented, as those fishing and farming villages were poor as well as picturesque. The boom in tourism has brought prosperity to many, and convenience to others by way of such 'luxuries' as water and electricity supplies.

PHOTO TIPS

Views such as that of
Vlacherna and Mouse Island
are irresistible, so make sure
you bring plenty of memory
cards and batteries for your
digital camera, or film if
you've not yet joined the
digital revolution. Try to
avoid taking photos in the
middle of the day, when the
sun casts harsh shadows on
buildings and details can be
lost. People are not at their
best either, when the sun is
bright and eyes are screwed
up against the light. A more
flattering light is that of early
morning or the often golden
hours of late afternoon and
early evening.

Pontikonissi ★★★

Pontikonissi or Mouse Island is the name of the further
of the two islets situated in the bay below Kanoni,
though it is sometimes incorrectly applied to the closer
one. The latter, joined to the mainland by a causeway,
is called Vlacherna.

On **Vlacherna** an immaculately white convent is
flanked by a single lofty tree standing taller even than the
bell tower. Fishing boats are tied along the causeway, and
with the blue sea, bobbing boats, white church, green tree,
the island of Pontikonissi behind and the mountain slopes
of southern Corfu in the distance beyond, it is little wonder
that so much photographic film has been exposed here.

What the photographs never show, of course, is the
car park that has been built to accommodate the endless
visitors, and the rather scruffy strip of land to the right
with, about 400m (437yd) away, the start of the airport
runway that was built on the lagoon. Nonetheless,
Vlacherna and Pontikonissi do provide a unique and
glorious view for the start and end of your visit to Corfu.

Boats from Vlacherna make the journey to and from Corfu Town hourly in
summer, and some will take interested
visitors on the short trip across to
Pontikonissi. Here a solitary church
hides among the vaguely mouse-shaped
trees, but the most interesting thing
about the islet is mythical. It is said to be
the petrified ship which, in Homer's
Odyssey, was wrecked by Poseidon,
causing Odysseus to be washed up on
the shores of Scheria. However, other
towns in Corfu, such as Ermones and
Paleokastritsa, also claim to be
Odysseus' landing point on the island.

Vido Island ★

This wooded island, prominent in the
waters of Corfu harbour, has been a
wildlife sanctuary since 1993. It is a

more peaceful place today than it was in the past. Once the hunting preserve of a Venetian count, it was occupied no less than three times over the centuries by forces attempting to take Corfu, who used it as a firing base. Later the British turned it into a penal settlement and later still it became a cemetery (*see* panel, page 19).

Boats run to the island from Corfu's Old Port every hour in summer, the last one returning in the early hours to allow visitors to take in an evening meal at the island's restaurant, with fabulous views of the night lights of Corfu Town.

To the east of Vido is the tiny islet of **Lazaretto**, also referred to as Gouvion and more clearly visible from the resort of Kondokali (*see* following chapter). Lazaretto may look attractive but it has a sad history, having been used in the Venetian period as a quarantine station for ships thought to be carrying the plague that badly affected Corfu. In more recent times, during the Greek Civil War which followed World War II, Lazaretto was used as a place of execution. Every 27 May a pilgrimage is made to the island by those families who lost loved ones, and flowers are placed in the bullet holes in the wall where the prisoners were shot.

Above: *The keen photographer will be challenged to find a new angle on this most photographed of scenes, below Kanoni.*
Opposite: *Peace and tranquillity in the convent on the island of Vlacherna.*

WHITE EGRETS

The airport runway, built into the Halikiopoulos Lagoon close to Corfu Town Centre, is good news for visitors and the tourist trade, but bad news for the white egret. This graceful bird sometimes winters in the lagoon and, with an estimated population of only 200 individuals, it is one of the most endangered species in Europe. About half the population has been counted on the lagoon at one time.

Corfu Town at a Glance

From **May–June** and **September–October** the sun is likely to be shining and the streets less crowded than at peak times, yet everywhere will be open. For local colour, visit at **Easter** (note that the Orthodox festival rarely coincides with Easter in western Europe), or at the time of one of **St Spiridhon's processions** (see page 39). **Carnival**, just before Lent, is also a colourful event, while in August the Feast of the Assumption is another major celebration.

The **international airport** (tel: 26610 30180) is about 1.5km (1 mile) south of the town centre and offers tourist information, car hire, snacks, a bar, duty-free shopping and currency exchange (open 09:00–02:00, when international flights are expected). Otherwise, visitors should have some euros available for a taxi as there is no public bus service into Corfu Town. However, a courtesy bus meets Olympic flights and takes passengers to the Olympic office on Polila, tel: 26610 38694.

Corfu Town is small enough to see **on foot**, with the occasional taxi if visiting, say, Kanoni, though this is also served by bus. The main **taxi rank** is on the Esplanade with others on Theotoki and San Rocco Square, and smaller ranks elsewhere (tel: 26610 33811). **Buses** serving the town and its suburbs can be picked up at the Esplanade and San Rocco Square. Unless you are visiting the rest of the island, **car hire** is best avoided because of parking and driving difficulties in the busy, narrow streets.

Note: all hotels in Kanoni suffer some airport noise during the day.

LUXURY

Corfu Holiday Palace, in Kanoni, tel: 26610 36540, website: www.corfuholiday palace.gr Set in woodland, with own beach, pool, bars and recommended restaurant; complimentary bus service to Corfu Town.
Corfu Palace, tel: 26610 39485, website: www. corfupalace.com Elegant hotel overlooking Garitsa Bay with beautiful gardens and views across to the Greek mainland; indoor and outdoor pools plus separate children's pool, sun terraces and many other facilities.

MID-RANGE

Cavalieri Hotel, tel: 26610 39041, website: www. cavalieri-hotel.com 4-star hotel; modern façade hides old-style hotel with character, near Esplanade and sea front; no swimming pool, roof garden with views.

Corfu Divini Palace, tel: 26610 38996, website: www.divanis.gr 4-star hotel with own pool and disco in Kanoni.
Arion, tel: 26610 37950. Fairly large 3-star hotel out of the centre, in the suburb of Anemomilos (the Mon Repos area), with gardens, swimming pool and sun terrace. Public bus to town centre stops outside.
Palace Mon Repos Hotel, tel: 26610 32783, fax: 26610 23495. Close to Mon Repos Lido, this 3-star hotel is 3km (2 miles) out of town. It has a garden and a restaurant serving local dishes.
Hotel Atlantis, tel: 26610 35560, e-mail: info@atlantis-hotel-corfu.com website: www.atlantis-hotel-corfu.com New, comfortable hotel, overlooking the harbour.
Bella Venezia, tel: 26610 46500, website: www. bellaveneziahotel.com Smartly restored old mansion; quiet but central and reasonably priced 2-star hotel.
Hotel Royal, tel: 26610 37512, fax: 26610 38786. Reasonably priced and ornately decorated 2-star hotel in Kanoni; three eye-catching linked swimming pools.

BUDGET

Hotel Ionion, tel: 26610 39915. 2-star hotel below the New Fortress; overlooks the harbour; drab exterior hides pleasant en-suite rooms.

Corfu Town at a Glance

Only the smarter Corfu restaurants take telephone bookings; where no number is given you cannot reserve by phone.

Aegli, tel: 26610 31949. Lovely setting on both sides of the Esplanade, good traditional food that is not too outrageously priced.

Aleko's, in the small harbour by the Old Fort. Simple food but a great location.

Il Giardino, tel: 26610 30723. Almost opposite the Archaeological Museum; expensive and smart Tuscan restaurant.

Hrissi Kardia, Sevastianou. Noisy taverna with good grilled food; always full of locals.

Mouragia, Arseniou 15, tel: 26610 33815. Great little *ouzerie* doing good meze and packed with Greeks at weekends.

Poulis, Spirou Arbanitaki. Tucked away on a side street off Theotoki is this typical Corfiot grill.

Rex, tel: 26610 39649. Opened in 1932, with Corfiot, Greek and international dishes; fine wine list.

Rocco Restaurant, basic and cheap; Greek and other dishes, right in the centre on San Rocco Square.

Spiros, Guilford Street (southeast of Town Hall); busy Corfiot grill-cum-takeaway.

Tenedos, Solomou 1, tel: 26610 36277. Friendly spot, often with live music and delicious specials such as lamb in a lemon sauce.

Venetian Well, Kremasti Square (near the Cathedral), tel: 26610 44761. Delightful atmosphere and excellent, good-value Corfiot food; menu changes daily.

Yisdhakis, Solomou (off N Theotoki). Serves authentic local food.

The smartest area for cafés is the Liston. For a more authentic local atmosphere try the establishments in and near San Rocco Square.

A leisurely trot around Corfu Town in a horse and buggy is a very popular option among holiday-makers. Corfu Town is also the best place from which to plan your ferry trips to other islands.

All Ways Travel, tel: 26610 33955, fax: 26610 30471, website: www.corfu allwaystravel.com

Corfu Infotravel, tel: 26610 41550 / 25792, fax: 26610 23829.

Eurocorfu Travel, tel: 26610 46886, fax: 26610 46887.

Sailing Holidays Travel, tel: 26610 32273.

Ambulance, tel: 166

Bus Timetables, tel: 26610 39859 (local/Benitses/Dassia), or 26610 39985 or 30627, Green Bus (the rest of the island).

Corfu Climbing Club, tel: 26610 39481.

Corfu General Hospital, Polikhroniou Konstanda, tel: 26610 88200.

Corfu Tennis Club, Romanou (near Archaeological Museum), tel: 26610 37021.

Ferry Timetables, tel: 26610 32655.

Live entertainment, cultural evenings are held every Tuesday in summer at 20:00 in the Town Hall Square and other squares, featuring music and dancing.

NTOG (official National Tourism Office of Greece), temporarily closed; look for new office opening near Town Hall.

Police, tel: 100.

Port Police, tel: 26610 32655.

Post Office, the main branch of the post office is on Alexandras, open 07:30–20:00, Monday–Friday, tel: 26610 25544.

Tourist Police, tel: 26610 30265.

CORFU	J	F	M	A	M	J	J	A	S	O	N	D
MAX TEMP. °C	14	14	16	19	24	28	31	31	28	23	19	15
MIN TEMP. °C	5	6	7	9	13	16	18	18	16	13	10	7
RAINFALL mm	153	140	107	64	38	12	7	17	84	152	193	185
RAINFALL in	6.0	5.5	4.2	2.5	1.5	0.5	0.3	0.7	3.3	6.0	7.6	7.3
DAYS OF RAINFALL	17	15	15	12	9	5	2	3	7	12	16	18

3
The Northeast

The sweep of coast stretching from the northern suburbs of Corfu Town to the resorts that nestle below Mount Pantokrator is the most touristy area of the island, with boisterous towns such as **Ipsos** and **Pyrgi**, where anything goes in summer, and also some more family-based resorts such as **Kommeno** and **Gouvia**. This entire stretch of coastline is highly developed and the former traditional holiday villages, such as **Kondokali**, have now been all but overrun. **Ipsos** typifies this development, offering a thin string of pebble beach along the very busy coastal road, lined with bars, nightclubs, souvenir shops and fast-food establishments. The town does, however, boast one of the island's main diving centres.

At **Pyrgi**, situated approximately 16km (10 miles) north of Corfu Town, the coastal road continues around the bulge of the island while an inland road snakes over the western flank of the highest peak, **Mount Pantokrator** at 906m (2973ft), towards the northern coast. A detour inland goes through the old, picturesque village of **Strinylas** from where a good road leads up to the mountain's summit, affording spectacular views. A number of perfectly drivable roads go through mountain villages almost to the summit, making for pleasant country driving. The green slopes are rich in plant life, particularly orchids.

The resorts that form an almost unbroken chain around the northeastern coast of the island have an entirely different feel from the holiday centres that line

DON'T MISS

★★★ Kalami: village with literary connections.
★★★ Kouloura: a peaceful resort with a delightful harbour.
★★★ Mount Pantokrator: Corfu's highest peak with magnificent views.
★★★ Roda, for a beautiful stretch of beach.
★★ Barbati: located in a beautiful setting under Pantokrator.
★★ Kassiopi: a lively holiday resort.
★★ Antinioti Lagoon, for a glimpse of Corfu's wildlife.

Opposite: *Barbati's magnificent setting is typical of northeast Corfu.*

Map labels (clockwise/reading order):

Sokraki, **Ano Korakiana**, Agios Markos, Pyrgi, Spartilas, Barbati, Barbati Beach, Skripero, Kato Korakiana, Ipsos, Ipsos Pyrgi Beach, KAROUSSADES, PALEOKASTRITSAS, Dassia, Akra Kefaloipsos, Dassia Beach, 0   4 km, 0   2 miles, Sgombou, Akra Kommeno, Tsavros, Kommeno Beach, Gouvia Bay, Gouvia Beach, **IONIAN SEA**, Gouvia, Lazaretto, Vido Island, Kondokali, Tembloni, CORFU (KERKYRA), Akra Sidheros, Ropa, **Ropa Plain**, Evropouli, Potamos, Corfu Golf & Country Club, Ermones, Kefalovrisso, IOANNIS KAPODISTRIAS INTERNATIONAL AIRPORT, Kellia, Vatos, 390 m, 377 m, Kombitsi, Limni Halikiopoulos, Garitsa Beach, Mirtiotissa Beach, Kastania, **Kanoni**, **N**, Pelekas, Vlacherna Pontikonissi, Glifada Beach, Kalafationes, Yiros, **Perama**, Kinopiastes, Sinarades, BENITSES

the bay north of Corfu Town. It is worth pressing on up the coast at least as far as **Kalami**, a quiet resort now somewhat developed, but where it is still possible to imagine the time when Lawrence Durrell wrote *Prospero's Cell* at the White House here. A little further on are the even quieter villages of **Koulouria** and **Agios Stefanos**, with lovely views towards Albania, a mere 2km (just over a mile) away at this point. Around the point of the coastal bulge is **Kassiopi**, a bustling tourist resort filled with bars and souvenir shops.

There is a great variety of fine scenery in the far north and good walking too. Here you will find the longest single stretch of **golden sand** on the island, the wetlands of the **Antinioti Lagoon** for birdwatchers, and busy resorts such as **Akharavi** and **Roda**. This area will probably appeal to those visitors who wish to go out and about while also enjoying water sports and some evening entertainment.

NORTH OF CORFU TOWN
Kondokali ★

Lying only approximately 6km (4 miles) to the north of Corfu Town, Kondokali is – not surprisingly – heavily developed for tourism. This village is situated in an ideal spot, at one end of the grand sweep of **Gouvia Bay** with its offshore island of Lazaretto (see below) and, beyond that, the mountainous Albanian mainland. A promontory juts out to sea, helping to provide shelter for the yachts moored in the excellent marina here. A part of the wooded headland is given over to the elegant, luxury class **Kondokali Bay Hotel**, which offers a comprehensive range of facilities, including air conditioning, satellite TV, its own sports facilities, salt-water swimming pool and nightclub.

The islet of **Lazaretto** was used as a place of execution for communist rebels who opposed the government during the Greek Civil War (see page 55). This conflict broke out only three months after the liberation of Greece from the occupying German forces of World War II, and was not resolved until 1949 after the loss of half a million lives.

Holiday development has so overrun the village of Kondokali that very little remains of the old town – a short street with a few traditional bars is all there is. There are, however, several good restaurants as well as a few hotels and tourist shops.

The village itself is off the main coastal road, with bars, tavernas and shops lining its own main street. Several smaller streets lead down to thin strips of **pebbly beach**, packed in summer and providing a wealth of **water sports**. The bay is very sheltered thanks to the two pincers of land that protect it from the Ionian Sea, and the water is quite shallow here. With several buses per day to and from Corfu Town, Kondokali makes a good spot for those who want a lively holiday with lots to do, and who don't mind the fact that there is little real Greek feel to the place. The resort of Gouvia, located just 5 minutes from Kondokali, offers a more family-based atmosphere.

'GREEK NIGHTS'

Anyone visiting Corfu on a package holiday is sure to be offered the chance to attend one of the organized 'Greek nights', for a '**typical Greek evening**'. Perhaps 'exaggerated' rather than 'typical' would better describe these occasions, but they are nevertheless terrific fun if you like your nights out to be raucous. They generally take place at inland hill villages, where the income is no doubt very welcome to the taverna owners. There will be plentiful food, endless drink and a chance to hear *bouzoúki* music and to watch – and participate in – some traditional Greek dances.

CATCH THE BUS

No visit to Corfu is complete
without a trip on a local bus.
Buses provide a very cheap
way to get around the island,
often travelling on the beautiful coastal roads or through
the highly dramatic scenery
of the interior. They are sure
to provide some fun or
drama – someone will almost
miss the bus or go past their
stop, or some of the passengers will get involved in a
heated debate. In summer
the driver will cram as many
people inside the bus as possible – and then a few more.
You can flag a bus down if
you're not at the official stop,
and most drivers will drop
you anywhere you like.

DRIVERS BEWARE!

Greeks are charming people
until they are behind the
wheel of a car. Male drivers
often become rude and
aggressive, and act as if
theirs is the only car which
has any right to be on the
road, sticking to the middle
and ignoring the possibility
that someone might be coming the other way. You will
discover that a Greek driver
does not hesitate to overtake
when going uphill and a
blind bend is approaching.
The visiting driver can only
take extra care – and perhaps
offer a prayer to St Spiridhon.

Gouvia ★★

Just a couple of kilometres beyond Kondokali, in a
rural setting among olive groves and cypress trees,
Gouvia stands in an attractive location at the heart of
its own natural harbour. There are splendid views out
to sea and also of Mount Pantokrator to the north,
where Corfu's coast swings dramatically eastwards
below the peak. This is more of a **family resort** than
Kondokali, quieter and with safe bathing from a curving sand and shingle beach, which offers the usual
facilities of sunbeds and umbrellas for hire, as well as
various popular water sports such as paragliding and
water-skiing. This is in fact one of the biggest resorts
on the eastern coast of Corfu, attracting visitors from
all over Europe.

Like Kondokali, Gouvia has its own **marina** at
the southern end of the village – work began about 20
years ago under a scheme by the Greek tourist authorities to improve the quality of some of its marinas to
international standards, and work at Gouvia was completed a few years ago.

The Turkish troops of Suleiman the Magnificent
needed no such facilities in 1537 when they attempted
to invade Corfu at this point on the coast. Close to the
marina are the remains of a Venetian arsenal and ship-
yard, built after the Turkish siege of 1716. Now roofless,
its massive arches nevertheless evoke the arrogance of a
power that had dominated the Mediterranean for centuries. In more recent times, Gouvia Bay was used as a
naval base by another nation – the French fleet was here
in World War I.

As well as the marina, which draws hundreds of
yachts from all over the Mediterranean, Gouvia has
several hotels, some restaurants serving traditional
Greek dishes, and a few rooms to let. Most of the shops
are concentrated along one short, narrow street in the
centre of the town.

For those who wish to get out and about, excursions
from Gouvia include boat trips around the bay and also
renting a car to explore the local countryside.

Kommeno ★★

One of the lesser-known resort areas along this stretch of coast, and not even mentioned in some guidebooks, Kommeno appeals to some people for its very **lack of tourist facilities** – at least compared to the other resorts nearby. It clusters around its own small bay, facing Kondokali on the opposite side of the larger Gouvia Bay. It has several small sandy beaches, which have been purpose made, some for the use of guests at the luxury hotel on one of the cape's headlands. There are other hotels and some shops and tavernas scattered around, but Kommeno is a cape and a bay rather than an actual old village – one of the reasons development has been slow. Kommeno lies well away from the busy coastal road, surrounded by woodland; visitors need to have the use of a car or be prepared to walk 3km (2 miles) to Gouvia or 2km (just over a mile) to Dassia for access to buses into Corfu Town.

Below: *Water-sports centres, like this one at Dassia, can be found in most of the major resorts.*

BEST BEACHES

** **Gouvia:** a curve of sand
and shingle with safe bathing.
** **Kommeno:** offering a
choice of small sandy bays.
** **Ipsos** and **Pyrgi:** lovely
'Golden Mile' of beach if
you don't mind company.
** **Agios Spiridhon:** large
sandy beach, quiet in places
but can be busy in season.
** **Roda:** a bay which is
large enough for you to be
able to escape the crowds.
* **Barbati:** stony beach, but
in an impressive setting
below Mount Pantokrator.
* **Kaminaki:** shingle beach in
a typical Greek setting.

Dassia ★

Dassia is an increasingly popular resort. Large though the beach is, it still becomes very full indeed at the height of the season, with more and more visitors arriving as new hotels are built year after year. The two Chandris hotels which for a long time dominated the resort, with over 1000 beds between them, have recently been joined by several others, adding many more beds. Furnished apartments and rented rooms also abound. With **discos**, **bars** and **bustle**, it is not a resort for those who like peace and quiet and an early night.

Most of the hotels, bars, tavernas, cafés, supermarkets and souvenir shops run along either side of the busy coastal road, which cuts straight through the village and could be a drawback for families. However, the long strand of mostly **shingle beach** is away from the road, reached down narrow alleys and backed by olive groves, which help cut down the noise of the passing traffic. The word *dasos*, meaning 'forest', indicates the **wooded nature** of this region.

Slightly inland is the village of **Kato Korakiana**, the Corfu annex of the Greek National Gallery in Athens. It has a small, but interesting permanent collection, and changing exhibitions.

Ipsos and Pyrgi ★★

If you're looking for good old-fashioned fun in the sun, this could be the place for you. Once separate resorts, Ipsos and Pyrgi have now merged, giving an indication of their recent rates of expansion. They share a long curve of beach, a mix of sand and shingle, giving the resorts the title of '**The Golden Mile**'. At the height of the summer they are patronized almost exclusively by young, single Europeans, whose idea of a good holiday is to drink all night and spend the next day recovering. The British are very much in evidence, with British pubs, British breakfasts and fish and chip shops outnumbering the more traditional Greek places.

In early and late season, when there is room on the beach and the night noise is not quite so relentless,

YES AND NO

In Greek *ne* means 'yes' and
ochi 'no' (pronounced *neh*
and *oh-kee* or *oh-she* respec-
tively). Further confusion can
be caused by a common
Greek gesture that can look
like a nodding of the head in
agreement: a backward
movement of the head with a
raising of the eyebrows,
sometimes with an added
tutting sound, in fact means
a definite 'no'.

Ipsos and Pyrgi make a **good base** for those who don't necessarily fall into the young and single category. There are plenty of facilities, Corfu Town is only 14km (9 miles) away with regular bus services, the area behind the resorts is filled with pleasant paths through olive groves, and beyond these the slopes of Mount Pantokrator rise to give a glorious backdrop to this sweep of beach.

One drawback at **Ipsos** is that the main road runs right alongside the beach. Behind the southern stretch of this beach, a few old cottages and a church remain to remind people of the tiny settlements which used to be here. **Pyrgi** to the north has the sandier part of the beach. The resort marks, for the moment, the end of the near-continuous spread of development on this stretch of coast north of Corfu Town. Inland the road leads up to **Agios Markos**, a village devastated in the 1950s by a landslide. Homeless families were given land further down towards Pyrgi and resettled in what became New Agios Markos. This settlement became the nucleus of the modern resorts, a different world from the timeless rusticity only a short distance inland from the beach, the

Above: *Ipsos harbour has everything from rowing boats to luxury yachts.*
Below: *While the beaches may be packed, the back streets of Ipsos still have quiet picturesque corners.*

Above: *Expect to pay a few euros to rent a sunbed for the day.*

bars and the discos. Many old houses remain in the still picturesque upper village and there are two old churches, one of the 11th and the other of the 16th century, the latter's walls covered with frescoes also from the 16th century. From here you have a wonderful view back down over Ipsos Bay. Just beyond Pyrgi, a road branches off to the left from the main coastal road and corkscrews its way up towards the top of Mount Pantokrator.

Most summer visitors sunbathe and roister unaware of the history of the two villages, but in the past the 'Golden Mile' has witnessed scenes rather different from those of today. As at Gouvia, the Turks attempted to invade here, in 1537 and again in 1716. The name Pyrgi means 'tower', referring to the towers built behind the coast to give advance warning of any potential Turkish attacks from the occupied mainland. Ipsos ('height') is said to have been named to fool the Turks into believing that it might not be a good place to try to capture. If invaders came today, they would have a serious problem getting through the water-skiers, paragliders, pedaloes, windsurfers and swimmers, let alone up the beach where sunbathers carpet the sand.

Barbati ★★

Though only about 2km (just over a mile) beyond Pyrgi, Barbati is a very different place. It is much more of a **family resort** and ideal for those who prefer a quieter holiday. That is not to say that facilities are non-existent – there are plenty of **water sports** on offer, sunbeds for hire and boat trips to take. There are simply far fewer of them, while the village itself has only a handful of souvenir and other shops. Barbati has a more **impressive setting** than the resorts to the south, with the slopes of Mount Pantokrator rising through olive groves almost immediately behind the white-stone beach, which turns to a sandy shingle where the water laps.

The main road is some way above the village, while the gently shelving beach and the sheltered nature of the bay mean that the bathing is fairly safe – all 'pros' for families with children. There is plenty of shade under the trees, which reach almost to the water's edge in places, and which tend to hide the few hotels and other buildings around.

Below: *At Nissaki boats will take you on trips along the coast, often with a barbecue picnic included.*

Nissaki ★

By the time it reaches Nissaki, the coast road is well above the several beaches which make up this **small fishing village**. Access is on steep tracks down through the olive groves. The main bars and restaurants and the few shops are along the main road, while the principal beach is of shingle and has a few tavernas. Other quiet beaches and private coves are accessible if you don't mind a short walk and a scramble down goat tracks to get to them.

Opposite: *Boats are often the easiest way to reach small bays, such as this one at Agni.*
Below: *Even quiet resorts like Agni are likely to throb with the noise of motorboats as people try out the many water sports on offer.*

Even though Nissaki is smaller and quieter than other resorts, it is a rare place on this part of the coast which does not offer a range of water sports, and this is no exception. There is windsurfing, paragliding and water-skiing, while boats are available for private hire as well as offering organized trips to other resorts along the coast. Corfu Town, 22km (14 miles) away, can be reached by boat or by the regular bus service which takes about 40 minutes. There are six buses daily in high summer, and taking the first bus in and the last bus back allows you at least five hours in Corfu Town. Close to the bus stop is a minor road marked Viglatsouri, which eventually leads to the deserted village of **Sinies** – a stimulating but tough walk.

Kaminaki ★

Although the relentless holiday development peters out at Pyrgi, Kaminaki is the first village along this coast where a sense of the real **pre-tourism Corfu** prevails. Access is down a snaking road off the main coast road, and the bulk of what little accommodation the village has to offer is in self-catering apartments hidden away on the thickly wooded slopes. Many of these are sold as part of a package holiday, so potential visitors should be aware of the shortage of casual 'rooms to rent'.

The beach here is of fine white shingle, with a few cafés and tavernas. There are windsurfers and boats for hire, and water-skiing lessons are available. A couple of shops and another taverna slightly away from the beach just about complete the facilities. The bay here is close to the northern end of the beach at Nissaki, and there are good coastal walks; a track along the coast leads north to the next resorts: Agni, Kalami and Kouloura.

Agni ★

Agni is reached by a very steep road down from the main road, which at this point is about 60m (197ft) above the coast. This used to deter Greek drivers, who are not given to walking long distances in order to find places to swim and eat. The improved road now makes access easier and the beach busier. The handful of **tavernas** along the steeply shelving pebble beach have good reputations, and the famous Taverna Nikolas offers a service whereby diners are collected in its boat and returned home later in the evening (it can be booked in Kalami).

THE ANGLO-ALBANIAN INCIDENTS

In 1945–6 a series of battles took place in the Corfu Channel between the British Royal Navy and the communist forces of Albania, who had taken control of the country after wartime liberation. The channel was heavily mined by the Albanians, and the Royal Navy suffered its heaviest casualties after the end of World War II, particularly in 1946 when 44 sailors died in a single incident: they are buried with a memorial in the British Cemetery in Corfu Town. On 9 April 1949, the International Court of Justice of the United Nations gave its first decision, when it held Albania responsible for these incidents and awarded damages to Britain.

Right: *The dramatic colours of Corfu in summer are shown in the harbour at Kouloura: bright whites, deep blues and verdant greens.*

Kalami ★★★

The main road turns right into Kalami, and goes on to the neighbouring resort of Kouloura. Kalami's claim to fame in English-speaking circles is the **Durrell connection**. Lawrence Durrell wrote *Prospero's Cell* in 1939 in the White House at the southern end of the bay, now a taverna with some rooms to rent, including the one in which Durrell worked and which still contains his desk. Some sources mistakenly claim that this is the 'white house' in which the whole Durrell family lived, as described in Gerald Durrell's *My Family and Other Animals*. However, the 'Snow-white Villa' of that book is described as being 'perched on a hill-top among olive trees' – clearly not the White House at Kalami, which stands at the water's edge and which Lawrence Durrell rented for a while with a friend.

Literary connections apart, Kalami is a delightful small resort, its curving bay of coarse sand and shingle fringed at the back with cypress and olive trees. During the day it is popular with boat excursions and car drivers, but in

the evening it quietens down, though there is often **Greek dancing and music** at one or more of the handful of beach tavernas. For a small resort, its facilities are quite good, with car, bike, sea scooter and boat hire all available. Outside July and August, it would make the ideal spot for those who want a quiet, **genuinely Corfiot resort**. Buses run to Corfu Town from the Kalami-Kouloura junction.

Kouloura ★★★

The final resort along this coast, before the road stops heading east and swings to the north, is even less busy than Kalami. Kouloura has a much smaller beach, of rocks and pebbles, without even sunbeds for hire. Life tends to centre on the **attractive old harbour**, with its solitary taverna and a few boat trips on offer. The small harbour is surrounded by cypress trees and forms almost a complete circle in the larger circle of the bay: Kouloura means 'ring' (there is also a round biscuit called a *Kouloura*), the name deriving from the shape of the bay. Beyond the bay lies the mainland of Albania, only a couple of kilometres distant at this point.

Below: *Kouloura's rounded harbour still has as many local fishing boats as those bringing in day-trippers to this idyllic place.*

THE FAR NORTHEAST
Mount Pantokrator ★★★

At 906m (2973ft), Mount Pantokrator may not be
exceptionally high compared to peaks on the Greek
mainland or on other larger Mediterranean islands,
but to reach the summit still feels like an achievement,
especially if you have done it on foot. The reward is a
stunning view, over the bay to Corfu Town in the
south, across the straits to Albania in the east, and even
to Corfu's offshore islands in the distant northwest.
Away to the south, you might be able to see the small
islands of Paxi and Antipaxi, and it is said that on an
exceptionally clear day the Italian mainland is visible.
On the way up you may see some of Pantokrator's
many **orchids**, such as the easily recognizable spider
and monkey orchids. The many other flowers, including purple crocuses and golden-headed thistles, attract
large numbers of butterflies. Unfortunately there are
also multitudes of flies in places, so go prepared with
insect repellent .

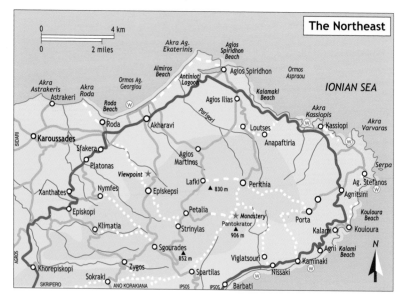

The mountain can be approached from near Pyrgi, or from a turn-off marked 'Loutses' roughly midway between Kassiopi and Akharavi. The road that goes to the summit is surfaced now and can be driven easily, with a few sharp bends to keep the driver paying attention. Parking at the top can be tricky – the nearer to the monastery you go, the harder it is to turn around. Directions are not really necessary, as the top is crowned by an **old monastery** and a rather more visible modern radio mast. In summer, you should take plenty of water and try to avoid the midday sun. In spring or autumn – and certainly in winter – don't attempt to go up if there are clouds around: the weather can change quickly on Corfu, so you should avoid the risk of getting lost in descending mist. In any case, always let someone know where you are going.

Agios Stefanos ★

A fishing village slowly developing into a resort, Agios Stefanos is a couple of kilometres off the main road, down a smooth but steeply winding road which tends to deter land-based visitors. However, day-trippers arrive by boat, so the idyll can be disturbed at any time during the day; the nightlife, on the other hand, being limited to a few bars and a handful of tavernas, will

---

FLORAL CORFU

If you are keen on botany – or just enjoy a **wild flower** display – April and May are the best months for exploring Mount Pantokrator. Greek fritillaries, saxifrage, anemones, borage, marigolds, irises, crocuses, gladioli and grape hyacinths all bloom then, along with the mountain's rich variety of **orchids**: toothed, man, monkey and both brown and yellow bee orchids are among the highlights. Elsewhere on the island, summer brings the flowering of the sea squill and sea daffodil, while in autumn an endemic snowdrop appears, the last flower of the year.

Above: *Boats are a way of life on all Greek islands, used for fishing, tourist trips or simply for transport.*

MOSQUITOES

Corfu is a hot and lush island with several lagoons – ideal mosquito territory. There are no malarial mosquitoes, so you won't require inoculations, but you may need protection, particularly in the evening and at night. A little insect repellent on wrists and ankles can help. The most effective deterrent in your bedroom is the plug-in device which slowly burns a small blue tablet overnight. Widely available all over Corfu, these are very effective. In the UK you can also buy personal solar-powered devices to carry on a keyring – these work well.

hardly attract the hordes. The main beach is large and pebbly and offers some water sports; for those who like even more **peace and privacy** there are quieter coves within walking distance.

At this point Corfu is at its closest to Albania, 1.7km (1 mile) away. Boats make the journey to Corfu Town, or you can walk up to the main road and flag down a bus. Greek bus drivers will happily stop to let people on and off even if there is no official stop.

Kassiopi ★★

Although Kassiopi is now a holiday resort town it has not yet lost sight of its traditional Corfiot origins, and tourist and traditional aspects manage to rub along together. **Fishing boats** still go out from the harbour each night, while the bars and discos are pulsating. Most of the development is in villas rather than hotels, so the attractive setting – between two headlands, below the mountain slopes and with views across the sea to Albania – has not been swamped with white concrete blocks.

The name is made up of *kassi* (meaning 'border'), and *opia* (meaning 'look-out point'). The Phaeacean god, Kassios Zeus, was the protector of such places, and it is believed that the white-walled town **Church of Kassiopitissa** now occupies the site of a Temple of Jupiter, which was once visited by the Emperor Nero. On one of Kassiopi's headlands lie the ruins of a 13th-century castle.

The beaches nearby are pebbly and involve a short walk over the headlands; the ones nearest the town offer a good range of **water sports,** with boats for hire. The town is just over an hour by bus from Corfu Town, with several buses daily in summer. The resort's appeal is mainly to younger holiday-makers, as the lack of an easy-to-reach beach discourages families; at the height of the season the fishermen will probably be back from their night's work before the bars in the centre have closed their doors behind the last customers.

Antinioti Lagoon ★★

At the northern tip of Corfu lies this lagoon, surrounded by reed-beds and a haven for **wildlife**. Several varieties of heron can be seen fishing here, the reeds hide warblers, and terrapins swim beneath the waves. Marsh harriers and nightingales are other residents. A church and a single taverna mark the sandy beach of **Agios Spiridhon**, though development is going on.

The headland here is a delightful place to explore: from the main beach a rough track leads off to the right to a quieter beach, while to the left is the channel connecting the Antinioti Lagoon with the sea. By crossing the bridge over this channel you come to another headland, more remote and usually crowd-free, ideal for not-too-strenuous walking as well as fertile territory for naturalists.

Akharavi and Roda ★★★

These two resorts stand close to each other on an unbroken stretch of **golden sand** extending for 8km (5 miles). By walking a short distance from the resorts, it is always possible to find a quiet, private spot on a beach of that size, and the sand shelves very gently in places, making ideal bathing conditions especially for young children.

The original village of **Akharavi** is a few hundred metres inland, and in the olive groves between it and the coast lie villas and some small hotels. You will still find fishermen here, but the village is increasingly turning to tourism.

Roda has already done so, with a greater number of hotels, including the large Roda Beach Village. It also has the remains of a 5th-century BC Doric temple, although most visitors will be more interested in the car and bike hire, tavernas, bars and water sports offered by both these pleasant but rather characterless resorts. Boat trips are available; regular destinations include Corfu Town, nearby resorts like Sidari and Kassiopi, and, further afield, Paleokastritsa and the off-shore islands.

The Northeast at a Glance

April/May to see orchids and other flowers if you're planning to walk on Mount Pantokrator; **July** and **August** for fun and sun; or **May/June** and **September** for a quieter holiday ... but still with sun.

The resorts closest to Corfu Town are easily reached by **taxi**, and all are served by a good **bus service** on the coast road. Some buses leave from the New Fortress bus station on Avramiou, the main street on the far side of the New Fortress from the port. One service goes to Ipsos/Pyrgi and another to Nissaki and Kalami. A service to Kondokali, Gouvia and Dassia leaves from San Rocco Square (Platia Theotoki).
To get further north, a bus runs several times daily from Corfu Town's New Fortress bus station and goes along the coast via Nissaki and Kalami to Agios Stefanos and Kassiopi. A different bus route from the same station goes inland to Akharavi and Roda. If you want to drive, there are many **car rental** offices in Corfu Town – international and local companies. Both the airport and Old Port area have a number. You can also hire mopeds or light motorcycles, but this mode of travel is not recommended because of the poor state of some minor roads and the unreliability of some of the machines rented out. There is a high accident rate.

Buses link the major resorts and villages, and **taxis** are available for shorter journeys. Although buses and taxis are the usual means of transport, **hitch-hiking** should not be too difficult on the busy coast road. All resorts offer **excursion trips**, often by boat to a remote beach, picking you up again later in the day. **Europcar** has rental offices in Akharavi, tel: 26630 29323. There are local car rental firms in all the resorts – even in some small places.

Akharavi
Ionian Princess, tel: 26630 63110, website: www.ionian princess.gr 4-star suites and 3-star rooms, close to beach; with large pool, sun terrace and gardens.
St George's Bay Country Club, tel: 26630 63203, website: www.stgeorgesbay.com Offers good 4-star rooms, but as self-catering accommodation.
Acharavi Beach, tel: 26630 63102, website: www. acharavibeach.com Pleasant small 3-star hotel, short walk from the centre; with pool and tennis courts.
Beis Beach, tel: 26630 63913. 3-star hotel, but larger than Acharavi Beach and with more facilities.

Dassia
Dassia Chandris and **Corfu Chandris**, tel: 26610 97100, website: www.chandris.gr Two old established 4-star

hotels with every amenity where guests benefit by the sharing of facilities.
Amalia, tel: 26610 93253. Small 2-star hotel, little way from the beach, but with good-sized pool and sun terrace.

Gouvia
Paradise, tel: 26610 91001, website: www.paradisehotel corfu.gr 3-star, medium-sized; quiet location some distance from beach and village centre.
Louvre, tel: 26610 91978, fax: 91979. Small, quiet, family-owned 2-star, 5 minutes' walk from the beach; own taverna.

Ipsos
Sunrise, tel: 26610 93414, website: www.sunrise-corfu.com Pleasant 3-star furnished apartments.
Mega, tel: 26610 93208, website: www.megahotel.gr Old-style 2-star hotel with good, inexpensive rooms.

Kassiopi
Apraos Bay Hotel, tel/fax: 266 30 98331. Slightly out of the centre, quiet and modern 3-star but built in traditional style.

Kommeno
Corfu Imperial, tel: 26610 88400. One of a handful of 5-star hotels. In splendid isolation on headland; private beaches, pool, gardens, good views.
Nefeli, tel: 26610 91033, website: www.hotelnefeli.com A lovely little hotel set in an olive grove above the centre of Kommeno.

The Northeast at a Glance

Kondokali
Kontokali Bay, tel: 26610 99000, website: www.kontokalibay.com 5-star with good sports facilities.

Nissaki
Nissaki Beach, tel: 26630 91232 5, website: www.nissakibeach.gr Large 4-star offering pools, sports, shops, disco, taverna.
Nissaki Apartments, tel: 26630 81806, website: www.falconcorfu.com Simple, but spacious rooms with lovely views of Corfu Town. Book per day or per week.

Pyrgi
Anna Liza Apartments, tel: 26610 93438. The only 4-star accommodation in Pyrgi.

Roda
Roda Beach, tel: 26630 64181. Large 3-star hotel with pools, own beach and gardens.
Roda Inn, tel: 26630 63358. Small 2-star hotel; central, by the sea, with taverna, bar and Greek dancing.

Agni
Taverna Nikolas, tel/fax: 26630 91136 / 91243 or book in Kalami. Delightful setting on quiet beach; essential to book a boat to get there and a table.

Akharavi
Maestro, serves local and international dishes in a picturesque location.

Dassia
Kiki's Fish Taverna, near the Elea Beach Hotel. Serves nothing but fish – which consequently tends to be good.
Taverna Castello, family-run taverna serving traditional dishes.

Gouvia
Steki, cheap and cheerful grill place on the main street.

Ipsos
Phoebus Restaurant, English-run with a Corfiot chef. Open all day.

Kalami
Dimitri's Bar, tel: 26630 91243. Traditional and international dishes; superb views; booking essential; transport provided.
White House Taverna, good traditional food.

Kaminaki
Spiro's Taverna, tel: 26630 91211. On the beach; serves Spiro's mother's home cooking.

Kassiopi
Little Italy, tel: 26630 81749. Southern Italian cooking, with a lovely little outdoor courtyard.
Szechuan, tel: 26630 81097. One of the few Chinese restaurants in the Greek islands, with a branch in Corfu Town.
The Three Brothers, tel: 26630 81211. Typical Greek taverna on the harbour, its

atmosphere not yet spoiled by the increasing tourist trade.

Kondokali
Takis Taverna, typical Corfiot taverna; traditional dishes.
The Viceroy Indian Restaurant, offers a rare chance to eat from a tandoori oven in Greece.

Roda
Roda Inn, tel: 26630 63358. Has a good restaurant which is also open to non-residents.

Agathi's Lace, tel: 26630 81315. Sells handmade lace and rugs in Kassiopi.
Corfu Divers, Kassiopi, is a PADI-registered diving centre, tel: 26630 29226.
Ionian Travel, on main road to Paleokastritsa, tel: 26610 99403, website: www.ioniantravel.gr Can help with accommodation and excursions.
Jet Ski Water Club, tel: 26610 91358. Runs water sports in Kondokali.
Leather Workshop, in Gouvia, tel: 26610 27288. For goods at factory prices.
Tassos Boats, in Kalami, tel: 26630 91251, website: www.kalamiboats.gr
The Travel Corner, in Kassiopi, tel: 26630 81220 / 81213, website: www.kassiopi.com Ferries and excursions.
Travel N S K, in Roda, tel: 26630 63471 / 63274, fax: 63274, website: www.nskcorfu.com Car hire, rooms, excursions, currency exchange.

4
The Northwest

Paleokastritsa has the reputation of being the most beautiful place on Corfu – and out of season, free of summer crowds, it is hard to disagree. Some enthusiasts go even further and call it one of Europe's most attractive spots, with its beaches, coves, woodlands, spectacular sunsets and steep winding streets.

The northwestern corner of the island has other attractions, giving you the choice of busy beach spots such as **Sidari**, quieter resorts like **Arillas**, or the even more get-away-from-it-all feeling provided by the **offshore islands** of Erikoussa, Othoni and Mathraki. History buffs can muse on the island's chequered past at the ruined fortress of Angelokastro, and lovers of landscape can marvel at the sunset-lit colours along the striated cliffs of Sidari and Peroulades. There are golden beaches like the one in beautifully situated **Agios Yioryios** for those who want to work on nothing more strenuous than their suntan, while the more energetic will enjoy the windsurfing at **Agios Stefanos**, the other water sports available just about everywhere, or a round of golf over 18 holes on the southern edge of the fertile **Ropa Plain**, courtesy of Corfu's only golf club

Sidari ★★

Sidari is centered on a lovely stretch of beach, which has resulted in the development of the village into a **busy package holiday resort**. If not quite as frenetic as the places nearer to Corfu Town, such as Benitses, it still has plenty of bars to make the place buzz at night.

DON'T MISS

★★★ Paleokastritsa: without question the most beautiful resort on Corfu.
★★★ The offshore islands for a glimpse of Greek island life, little changed over the years.
★★ Angelokastro: an imposing ruined fortress, with good views.
★★ Theotokos Monastery: best seen at sunset.
★★ Lakones: attractive inland village, noted for its views.

Opposite: *The black robes and long beards of Greek Orthodox priests are an imposing and frequent sight all over Greece.*

FOR THE YOUNG AND SINGLE

There are several Corfu resorts for which the word busy is an understatement, especially if visiting in July or August. In the height of summer they are taken over almost exclusively by young people, mainly from Britain, and mainly in search of drink, nightlife, sex and sunshine, not necessarily in that order. If this is what you want, the places to head for are Benitses, Kavos, Ipsos, Pyrgi and Kassiopi.

TAXIS

There is no shortage of taxis in Corfu Town, and each smaller town and village will probably have a taxi or two. In summer there may appear to be too few to go round, as licences are limited and the numbers are dictated by the needs of the local people rather than the requirements of summer visitors. Taxis are cheap, and locals often use them for long journeys. Although cars are metered, a fare may be negotiable for a specific journey, with the driver agreeing to pick you up again later in the day.

And the beach is ideal for young children, with shallow waters as well as the splendid sands.

The resort packs a lot into a small space. The one main street runs by the beach and carries the through traffic, but this is usually slow and light, while a parade of shops and tavernas between the road and the beach helps shield sunbathers from petrol fumes and noise. There are several hotels, but all are small and most are family-run. Other accommodation is in villas, both in the village and hidden in the **attractive groves of trees** inland.

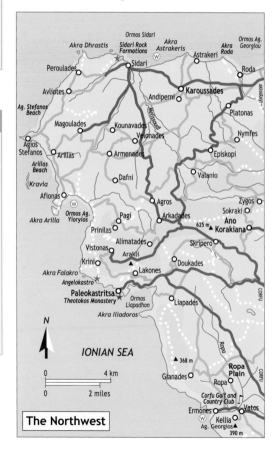

Opposite: *The Canal d'Amour in the rock formations at Sidari.*

Sidari has long been noted for its coves and limestone **rock formations**. There are plenty of quiet coves along the coast which can be reached on foot, on a boat trip or simply by paddling your own canoe or pedalo. Any number of other boat trips are available, to resorts such as Paleokastritsa, or to the offshore islands. There is a regular bus service to Corfu Town, and visitors can hire cars, motorcycles, bicycles, boats and even horses, to ride along the impressive, yellow sandstone cliffs or to explore the peaceful agricultural region behind Sidari for a glimpse of everyday Corfiot life. Sidari is one of the oldest known settlements on the island – archaeologists have unearthed the remains of a pre-Neolithic community dating back to about 7000BC.

BEST BEACHES
★★★ **Agios Yioryios:** picture-postcard golden stretch of sand.
★★★ **Paleokastritsa:** crowded, with no single best beach, but scenically stunning.
★★ **Agios Stefanos:** 2km of sand; idyllic out of season.
★★ **Sidari:** delightful but usually very crowded.

One popular feature of the resort is the so-called **Canal d'Amour**, a channel rather than a tunnel of love. This was formed between two large rocks in the bay, where the action of the sea on the soft sandstone produced a small tunnel, which the continued erosion eventually turned into a fully-fledged channel. You can believe whichever you prefer of the several different legends about it: that any person swimming in the channel while it is in shade will always be lucky in love; that any couple swimming through it, shaded or not, will stay together forever; or that any woman swimming through it will win the man of her dreams.

Peroulades ★

About 3km (2 miles) to the west of Sidari, in a striking setting, are the beach and handful of houses that make up Peroulades. The village is easily found by following the main road out of Sidari to the west, then taking the right-hand turning, signposted for the **Sunset Taverna**. As the name suggests, this is a popular evening spot, with high cliffs behind a beautiful sandy beach. The cliffs are a colourful mix of compressed clays and earth, at their best when the rays of the setting sun hit them. In front lies a **golden beach** of fine sand, delightful if you are there slightly out of season, though in high summer and especially at weekends it is rather too popular for its small size.

If the beach is full, many people seek a little space by walking north out of the village to explore Corfu's most northerly point, the promontory of Cape Dhrastis. This is composed of more cliffs surrounding small coves, with offshore rocks and distant views of the islands of Othoni, Mathraki and Erikoussa.

Agios Stefanos ★★

One of the two Corfu resorts called Agios Stefanos (the other is in the northeast), this is also sometimes referred to as **San Stefano**. It is ideal for those looking for a quiet holiday in a village that has not surrendered its essential

Opposite: Water provides entertainment – including fishing and sailing elegant flotilla yachts – for locals and tourists alike.
Right: The strange rock formations at Sidari ensure there are several protected coves to swim in.

Greekness to the tourist invasion. For the present Agios Stefanos remains a **fishing village**, with boats rocking in the small harbour below a church at the end of a sandy bay. There are beachside tavernas and water sports available – this westernmost point of Corfu is especially good for **windsurfing**. Accommodation is in a handful of villas, private rooms and apartments, and a few small hotels, though some are block-booked by tour operators

A surprisingly good bus service connects Agios Stefanos, at the end of the line, with Sidari (25 minutes) and on to Corfu Town (95 minutes) daily in summer. A short and enjoyable walk of less than an hour over the wooded headland brings you to the next resort to the south, Arillas.

Arillas ★

Arillas is another of the **relatively quiet** resorts in the northwest corner of Corfu, less accessible than other parts of the island though even Arillas clings on to its connection with the capital via a daily bus service that takes almost two hours through the inland mountain villages. The journey provides an opportunity to glimpse a little 'real' Corfiot life in these remote settlements, where the pace slows down to that of a donkey and there isn't a disco in sight. As in Agios Stefanos, the winds here on the western extremity of Corfu makes Arillas popular with windsurfers, and boards, boats and pedaloes can all be hired. The beach is mostly sand with some shingle, and runs for about a kilometre around the bay. There are several small hotels, bars and tavernas, and one or two discos.

TRULY RURAL

The villages in the hills behind the coastal resorts are worth taking the trouble to visit. They offer an opportunity to observe typical Corfiot rural life, unaffected by tourism – to the extent that, though most have a café, you can't bank on getting a meal. Even if you don't have a car, some of the buses to Corfu Town go through the villages, and a careful study of the timetables should enable you to spend a few hours exploring the villages and the mountains around.

The Offshore Islands ★★★

From many points along the northwest coast you can see three small islands, all of which can be visited from Sidari or on the ferry from Corfu Town. Day-trips are also possible in high season from other resorts including Kassiopi and Agios Stefanos. The day-trippers seldom venture further than the nearest beach, so even in high season the islands are probably the best chance you have in Corfu of **getting away from it all**. Facilities are limited, so if you plan to stay you need to make sure accommodation is available before you go and consider food supplies too.

The most popular of the three is **Erikoussa**, which has one small hotel and rooms to rent in the main village. This village – Erikoussa – boasts a glorious sandy beach, and there are others on the island, none more than a short walk away through the heather or the cypress groves. There are two more small villages inland, though neither of these has a taverna, the only one being in Erikoussa itself (on the beach), where you will also find a few shops and cafés.

To the west of Erikoussa is **Othoni**, the largest of the islands, which has slightly more by way of facilities but – with just a few mainly shingle stretches – lacks the attractive beaches of Erikoussa. The island offers good anchorage for visiting yachts, and there are several tavernas, shops, cafés and rooms to rent. A single road leads from the harbour to the solitary inland village, through quiet olive groves and pine woods, to the other side of the island and a few more remote but rocky beaches. There is also a well preserved medieval fort on one of the island's hilltops. Othoni has been identified with the island home of Calypso, the nymph who kept Odysseus captive for seven years in Homer's *Odyssey*; boat trips can be made to 'Calypso's cave'.

Southeast of Othoni is **Mathraki**, the smallest of the trio, with two tiny villages joined by a strip of road, a single taverna and just a few rooms to rent. The long sandy beach on the east coast is a nesting site for the rare loggerhead turtle, so camping here is forbidden. Though small, the island is green and appealing.

Agios Yioryios ★★★

It would be hard to better the setting for this small but growing resort, with its sandy bay guarded by two headlands and backed by green mountain slopes. The **excellent beach** runs for 3km (2 miles) and offers good windsurfing, with water-skiing and jet-skiing also available. The sheer size of the beach, the fact that part of it is not accessible by road, and the availability of other beaches nearby all mean that the resort has not yet been swamped by its increasing popularity. However, more small hotels are being built and there is no lack of bars and restaurants, so Agios Yioryios, delightfully situated as it is, may soon be transformed into a bustling beach playground. Meanwhile, for a magnificent view – a vast panorama back over the bay and the headland beyond – walk up the rough road towards the lovely hill village of **Pagi** (by which name the beach is also sometimes known), and through the tall cypress trees.

KEEP COOL

The sun in midsummer can be fierce, and also deceptive when one of the occasional cooling breezes is blowing. Here are some precautionary **hints**:

• Time spent in the sun's full glare should be increased gradually, and on the first few days try to avoid the dangerous hours between about 11:00 and 15:00.
• Don't forget that the sun is just as hot if you are standing in the street window-shopping, so apply sunscreen regularly, and reapply after swimming.
• In very hot conditions, drink plenty of water or soft drinks to replace body liquid, and avoid too much alcohol which causes dehydration and can bring on sunstroke.

Left: *There are several resorts that bear the name of Agios Yioryios, St George, but this one in the northwest is one of the most popular.*

Angelokastro ★★

Between Pagi and Paleokastritsa lies the village of
Makrades, and from here a path leads towards the
headland on which stand the ruins of the 13th-century
fortress of Angelokastro – the climb takes about 20
minutes. The fortress is named after **Michael II Angelos
Komnenos** who, as Despot of Epirus, ruled Corfu in
the 13th century and is believed to have finished the
building of the fortress, although its precise history is
uncertain. It is believed that its original purpose was as
a defence against Genoese pirates. One thing that is
known is that during the Turkish invasion of 1571, people from the surrounding villages sought safety in the
castle. When the main strength of the Turkish attack
had gone, the villagers emerged to drive the remaining
invaders off. The Turks sailed away to defeat at the
hands of Christian forces in the Battle of Lepanto in the
Gulf of Corinth.

From this impregnable spot – the fortress was never
taken – there are some marvellous **views** south to
Paleokastritsa and, when the weather is clear, even
across the island to the Old Fortress in Corfu Town: the
two fortresses used to warn each other of impending
attacks. There is not much left of Angelokastro, apart
from a few walls and a well preserved cistern. Nearby
are some hermit cells and caves (one housing a shrine)
and, on the hill's highest point, a chapel dedicated to
the Archangels Michael and Gabriel.

Paleokastritsa ★★★

This is both the most popular and most attractive resort on
Corfu's west coast. Many regard it as the most beautiful
spot on the whole island, and one of the first to fall for its
charms was **Sir Frederick Adam**, British High
Commissioner to the Ionian Islands in the early 19th century. Its appeal then lay in its steep wooded slopes, blue
sea and several lovely bays with bathing beaches. One
problem was its comparative inaccessibility, so Sir
Frederick had a road built to the village, with the osten-
sible purpose of erecting a military convalescent home

Left: *Dance displays like this may be put on for the benefit of visitors, but they still form a part of modern Greek life, with some very skilful practitioners.*

there. This was never built, but Sir Frederick now found it much easier to take his regular picnics in Paleokastritsa. Such illustrious travellers as Empress Elizabeth of Austria, Kaiser Wilhelm of Germany and the English writer and artist Edward Lear soon followed in his footsteps.

Today there are fewer trees and many more buildings, but the setting has lost none of its beauty. Paleokastritsa is more of a **family resort** than many on Corfu, as the swimming is safe in any of its three main coves – Agia Triada, Platakia and Alipa – and off other minor beaches around, although the waters here are notably cold. The beaches are a mix of sand, pebble and shingle, most of them served by a taverna and other facilities – boat trips, water-skiing, canoes and a diving school – in summer. From the harbour you can take boat trips along the coast to look at the many grottoes in the vicinity, and out around the Rock of Kolovri, which – like Mouse Island off Kanoni – is said to be the petrified ship of Odysseus.

GREEK DANCING

It is the unlucky visitor who will not see at least one example of Greek dancing on a visit, whether staged or spontaneous. It is one of the oldest of Greek art forms, and shows no signs of dying out. Greek dances can be either *syrtos* (shuffling) or *pidiktos* (leaping), both being performed in a circular manner, though the circle is not always evident when the number of dancers is small. Some series of movements can be very complicated, but the visitor who tries to follow them will be heartily applauded. Greeks need little encouragement to dance.

PRESSING BUSINESS

In your explorations on Corfu you will almost certainly come across large circular stones with a small hole in the middle, lying abandoned. These are **old olive presses**. The olives were placed on the flat stone, while a similar but vertical stone was turned in a circle by a horse or donkey to press out the oil. Most villages had their own press; everyone used it and then received their share of the oil produced, which they would store at home in wooden barrels to see them through the year until the next harvest. Today this laborious task is done in electric presses.

The palace of Alcinous, king of the Phaeacians and father of Nausicaa who discovered Odysseus after his shipwreck, is reputed to have stood nearby. According to another legend, the Rock of Kolovri is the ship of an Algerian pirate intent on looting the monastery on the headland (*see* page 89). As the ship approached the shore, it was turned to stone in answer to the prayers of the Abbot. Today the rock is the haunt of seabirds.

The town itself now has well over a dozen hotels to choose from, plus villas and rooms to rent. Anyone who is not fully fit should note that some streets are very steep. There is no lack of bars and tavernas and, while it does not attract young single holiday-makers, Paleokastritsa's popularity makes it a place to avoid if your aim is to get away from it all. That having been said, there are quieter beaches a short walk away, and the town's spectacular location does make it a good base for walkers.

Left: *Church bells and bougainvillaea: this scene at the Theotokos Monastery is repeated throughout Greece.*
Opposite: *Whether your preference is a pedalo or a speedboat, even small beaches like this one at Paleokastritsa offer a good choice of water sports.*

Theotokos Monastery ★★

One of Paleokastritsa's headlands is the high perch of the Theotokos Monastery, also known as the Monastery of Panayias Paleokastritsas. A good time to visit is towards **sunset**, when most day-trippers have left and the sea and bays are aglow with the last of the golden-pink light: the monastery stays open until 20:00 every day. The first monastery on this site is thought to have been built in 1228, but the present buildings date from the 17th and 18th centuries. It is thought that in the Middle Ages the monastery was linked to the fortress of Angelokastro on the steep hill behind (*see page 86*). A monk often greets visitors with a glass of cold water drawn straight from the well, although the monastery is

> #### DRESS SENSE
>
> Most monasteries and convents will refuse admission to visitors who are not respectfully dressed. This can come as a surprise to those who are used to the casual approach to dress that is the norm on Corfu. But these are holy places, and it causes offence if visitors arrive in little more than brief swimsuits. Men should wear long trousers and women should wear skirts and avoid bare shoulders, although in some places shorts may be acceptable. It is better to be cautious and wear (or carry) suitable clothing, than to travel some distance to see a religious building and be unable to enter. If in doubt make enquiries before setting out.

Above: *Admission to monasteries like this one at Paleokastritsa is usually free, but a small donation, made perhaps by buying and lighting a candle, will be appreciated to help pay for the upkeep.*

---

no longer active and the monks' cells are empty. There is a flagged courtyard, lemon trees and an atmosphere of tranquillity. The **church** has an unusual painted and carved ceiling and a fine collection of icons. There is also a small **museum** with an eclectic display of shells, bones, icons and old books, an old olive press and large gardens where you can escape the heat of the sun.

Lakones ★★

Lakones is visited chiefly for its **superb views** over Paleokastritsa, but is itself an attractive hillside village clinging to the slopes of Mount Arakli, one of Corfu's highest peaks at 505m (1657ft). It has one narrow main street, through which a steady string of tour buses pass bearing day-trippers to its more famous neighbour. There are any number of tavernas, each allegedly offering the best views in the village – and priced accordingly. In fact the best view is outside Lakones at the Bella Vista café. This delightful if busy spot has a view perhaps only rivalled by the sight of Vlacherna and Pontikonissi at Kanoni. Lakones makes an excellent base for those who enjoy **walking**. There are rooms to rent in the village, and a choice of excellent walks.

The Ropa Plain ★

South of Paleokastritsa is a long undeveloped stretch of coast, inaccessible by road because of a range of hills, although boat trips will take sunbathers to some of its beaches. The next major resort, Ermones (*see page 94*), is about 10km (6 miles) south, the gap being filled inland by the flat and fertile Ropa Plain, a region of corn fields, vines, fruit and vegetable production and dairy farming. This was once marshland noxious with malaria-carrying mosquitoes until the occupying Italians drained it some 50 years ago. The plain is watered by the Ropa River, and its lushness is such that it is the site of the Corfu Golf and Country Club with Corfu's only **golf course**. The clubhouse features a bar and restaurant open to non-members, and horse riding is also available at the Ropa Valley Riding Stables based here.

The Northwest at a Glance

Midsummer if you like it busy, **May/June** or **September** for more peace and more space.

A good **bus service** from the New Fortress Square station links Corfu Town with Paleokastritsa, while another service runs from the same station to Sidari, Peroulades and Agios Stefanos.

Apart from the bus service, use **taxis** for short hops and **excursions/boats** to visit other resorts. Regular boats visit the offshore islands.

Agios Yioryios
Costas Golden Beach, tel: 26630 96208. 2-star; attractively placed with pool; most rooms overlook the beach.
Hotel Belle Helene, tel: 26630 96201, website: www.belle helenehotel.gr Clean but simple beachside hotel, with taverna and pool attached.

Liapades
Elly Beach Hotel, tel: 26630 41455. Lovely bay setting.

Paleokastritsa
Akrotiri Beach, tel: 26630 41275, website: www.akrotiri-beach.com Good 4-star; own pool, bars, disco and games.
Oceanis, tel: 26630 41229 / 30. A medium-sized 3-star with pool, restaurant and Greek music and dancing.

Paleokastritsa, tel: 26630 41207. Large 3-star with pool, children's playground, restaurant and nightclub.

San Stefano
Romanza, tel: 26630 51762. Family-run, furnished apartments with restaurant and pool.

Sidari
Mimosa, tel: 26630 95363. 2-star; close to the beach, with restaurant and snack bar.
Sidari Beach, tel: 26630 95215. 2-star; on a beach away from the town centre with restaurant and basic facilities.

Agios Yioryios
Delfini, has a delightful terrace and offers fresh local fish and lobster.
Taverna Afionis, good honest Greek taverna at the north end of the beach.

Lakones
Bella Vista, on the edge of the village, offering unrivalled views and Corfiot cooking.

Paleokastritsa
The Rock, tel: 26630 41233. Superbly situated on the rock that gives it its name, and serving good fresh dishes.

Peroulades
Sunset, Sidari road, tel: 26630 95334. Specializes in oven-cooked and spit-roast dishes.

Ropa Plain
Livadi Country Club, Greek,

English and French cooking, with an emphasis on game.

Sidari
Oasis, generally considered the resort's best restaurant, though out of the centre.

Mike's Water Sports, at Paleokastritsa, tel: 26630 41510, fax: 26630 41486. Books excursions and rents out water-sports facilities.
San Stefano Travel in Agios Stefanos, tel: 26630 51910, website: www.san-stefano.gr Can help with every aspect of your stay here.
Sellas Travel in Sidari, tel: 26630 995226 / 95494, fax: 26630 95311 / 95591, e-mail: sellastr@otenet.gr Helpful agency organizing excursions and boat trips to the islands.
Vlasseros Horse Riding Club, tel: 26630 95695.

Corfu Diving, in Paleokastritsa, tel: 26630 41604. Gives scuba diving lessons.
Corfu Golf Club, tel: 26610 94220, fax: 210 6923028, website: www.corfugolfclub. com An 18-hole, 72-par championship course.
Nearchos Cruises in Sidari (contact Sellas Travel, above) do cruises to the offshore islands and other destinations.
Ropa Valley Riding Stables, based at the Golf and Country Club, tel: 26610 94220. Offers hires for beginners or experienced riders.

5
The Centre and South

The eastern and western coastlines of the centre – Corfu's slim waist – could hardly be more different in the way they have developed. The east coast has a straight stretch of good road which runs for about 10km (6 miles) to the south of Corfu Town, and is lined by lively resorts not as close together as their counterparts on the coast to the north of the capital, but just as popular. In **Benitses** the south can boast its own busy package holiday resort, not quite as brash these days as it moves up-market with its new marina. Nearby is the bizarre palace of Elizabeth of Austria, the **Achillion**. The road finally turns inland as it reaches the smaller villages of **Moraitika** and **Messongi**.

The cliff-lined central west coast has no such convenient road – going from one resort to the next often involves a roundabout journey – so that between tourist resorts like **Ermones** and **Glifada** you will find quiet coves, accessible only on foot or by boat, and some of the best sandy beaches on the island.

Corfu's southern extremity has only one resort, **Kavos**, for those who like things wild and loud at night. Otherwise the beach resorts are small and well separated, like **Agios Yioryios**, good for beach-lovers, and **Petriti**, little more than a fishing village with a bit of tourism. The main road runs down the centre of this narrowing strip, seldom far from a turning that leads down to a beach, often deserted. There are many inland farming villages to explore, plus **Lake Korission** (Limni Korissia), a peaceful haven for wildlife. At the southern tip are the white sand beaches of **Cape Asprokavos**.

DON'T MISS

★★★ Mirtiotissa: one of the island's best beaches.
★★★ The Achillion: bizarre, but unique.
★★★ Lake Korission: good beaches and wildlife areas.
★★ Benitses: the archetypal sun 'n' fun tourist resort.
★★ Pelekas: attractive hill town, with Kaiser's Throne.
★★ Sinarades Folk Museum: the only one on Corfu.
★★ Kavos: a raucous resort.
★★ Petriti: pleasant, not over-developed fishing village.

Opposite: *Spilio is typical of Corfu's mountain villages, hardly touched by tourism.*

HITCH-HIKING

Hitch-hiking is legal in Corfu, and lifts should not be too hard to come by as Greek drivers are generally helpful. However, cars and vans are frequently full of friends and relatives being transported here and there; also as the basic Greek motor insurance policy does not cover accidents many otherwise willing drivers will not take the risk of a potentially costly accident. But patience should pay off, even if your lift is in the back of a bumping van on a bag of watermelons, with sheep as your fellow travellers.

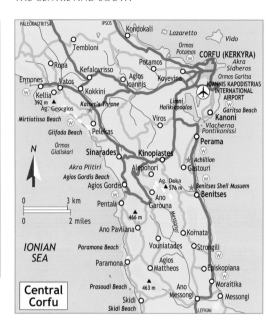

Central Corfu

OFF THE BEATEN TRACK

Corfu is a good place for walking, as it normally misses the extreme midsummer heatwaves that frequently strike Athens and the Aegean Islands. However, walkers should always be prepared for the chance of rain and be aware that mists can come down without warning on the higher slopes of the hills. On the whole, the holiday-makers attracted to Corfu want to do little more than lie on a beach during the day; as a result those few foreign visitors who take the trouble to visit the more remote villages are treated all the more hospitably by the villagers.

THE CENTRE
Ermones ★

On the edge of the Ropa Plain and a convenient base if you want to combine time on the beach with trips to the nearby **golf course** (see page 90), Ermones is a busy little resort, its bay overlooked by the bungalows of the Ermones Beach Hotel. The beach is a mix of sand, shingle and larger rocks, and in summer there seem to be as many people in the water as there are pebbles on the shore. Facilities include water-skiing, canoeing, pedaloes, paragliding, boat hire, boat trips and scuba diving. If **water sports** and golf are not enough, there are four tennis courts open to the public at the Ermones Beach Hotel, which is reached by funicular from the back of the beach. This is not an ideal place for children: apart from the frantic water sports and the shingle surface, the beach shelves quite sharply.

Ermones boasts two legends (suspiciously similar to those recounted in Paleokastritsa up the coast, see page

88). The largest of the rocks in the bay is said to be a pirate chief who was turned to stone for attempting to steal an icon from the church; some prefer to see it as a petrified nun. It is also claimed that it was here, where the Ropa River reaches the sea, that Odysseus was washed ashore naked in the **Odyssey**. Homer's hero had just escaped from the amorous nymph Calypso (whose home is said to have been on the offshore island of Othoni) when Poseidon turned his ship to stone. He reached the beach to be found by Nausicaa, the Phaeacian king's daughter, who had been washing some clothes in a nearby spring with her handmaidens. Ermones does have a convenient freshwater spring, and other evidence suggests that Homer may well have had Ermones in mind as the setting for this part of his epic tale – sufficient for one of the tavernas here to have named itself the Nausicaa. There are a number of other places to get food and drink plus two hotels.

Below: *Ermones has its Homeric connections, though most people are happy just to lie on its beach.*

Opposite: *Flotilla sailing is popular in the Ionian Sea, allowing holiday-makers the freedom to tie up at appealing small harbours.*

Vatos ★

For people based at Ermones, a popular walk is the 2 kilometres (just over a mile) to the inland village of Vatos, which has some rooms to rent, a few shops and two tavernas. There is a camp site (also called Vatos) situated about a kilometre outside the village. Cut off from the coast by the 392m (1286ft) slopes of **Mount Agios Yioryios**, Vatos is an attractive place to visit with its small whitewashed houses, and provides a peaceful contrast to the busy beaches. The path up from the village offers a great view over the plain and the coast.

Mirtiotissa ★★★

'During the afternoon ... I slip down to the house of the peasant family and borrow the Count's placid little mare, which will take me through the vineyards and woods to what is perhaps the loveliest beach in the world. Its name is Myrtiotissa.' So wrote Lawrence Durrell in *Prospero's Cell*, and the beach is undoubtedly beautiful, with the cliffs dropping sheer to the 'lion-gold' sand and the rocks ('pitted and perforated ... full of sea-water and winking

THE CORFU TRAIL

In May 2001, **Hilary Whitton Paipeti**, an Englishwoman now living on Corfu, led a guinea pig group of walkers along the Corfu Trail. Hilary first came to Corfu as a holiday rep in the early 1980s, but fell in love with the island so much that she has been here ever since. In addition to publishing and writing many of the local information magazines that you might find in your holiday resorts, Hilary is a keen walker and has also published books on Corfu's walks. The Corfu Trail is no ordinary walk, though. The idea came from Hilary's father, who suggested she

should organize a long-distance footpath through the whole of Corfu, the island's equivalent of Britain's Pennine Way. Hilary thought it was a wonderful idea, if rather daunting, but she was fired by a desire to take more holiday-makers to some of the inland villages, where populations had been dwindling and locals missed out on the tourist boom that made the coastal places so much more prosperous. And so the Corfu Trail was born. The Trail runs for about **220km** (137 miles) from the southernmost point of Corfu at **Cape Asprokavos** to the northernmost point near

the **Antinioti Lagoon**. The whole trip should take about **10 days**, doing 4–6 hours walking a day without pushing yourself. Anyone can arrange to do the Trail for themselves, and Hilary has written a guide to it which you will find in local bookshops and tourist offices, but it does take some planning. Instead you can book it all through Aperghi Travel in Corfu Town (tel: 26610 48713, e-mail: aperghi@travelling.gr), who will not only book the accommodation, but arrange for your luggage to be transferred each day and give you a copy of Hilary's book too.

fishes') adding a touch of drama to
the remote setting. It was difficult to
get to in Durrell's day, but the track
has since been greatly improved
and now a road zigzags down from
near Vatos, signposted for the
Monastery of Mirtiotissa (Our Lady
of the Myrtles) from which the
beach takes its name. Inappropri-
ately for somewhere so named, the
southern section is now a **nudist
beach**. The nearby **monastery**
(open 08:00–13:00 and 17:00–
20:00) retains a secluded dignity in
the midst of a grove of cypress,
olive and banana trees. It was
originally built in the 14th century
when a monk is said to have found
an icon of the Virgin Mary in one of
the myrtle bushes here, but the present buildings are more recent.

The beach itself is only a narrow stretch of sand and there are
no facilities other than a few snack
bars. Despite this, and the relative
difficulty of access, it is becoming increasingly popular
and can be very crowded. There is a taverna with some
rooms to rent partway along the road down to
Mirtiotissa. While it is possible to drive the whole way
down to the beach since the road was improved, it is
steep and not a little nerve-racking; you may prefer to
walk the final stretch.

Glifada **

This very attractive 2km (1 mile) stretch of sandy beach
is reached by a steep, winding road that cuts its way
through the cliffs. Glifada is not so much a resort as a
beach that has sprouted facilities, and a recent improve-
ment in the road can only encourage the development.
Two large hotels dominate the area, the luxurious Louis

BEST BEACHES

★★★ **Mirtiotissa:** the loveliest
beach in the world? Perhaps
not that, but certainly pretty.
★★★ **Lake Korission:** many
kilometres of golden sand
dunes and wildlife.
★★ **Agios Gordis:** headlands,
hills, olive groves and several
sandy stretches.
★★ **Glifada:** 2 kilometres of
sand and a handful of tavernas on an excellent beach.
★★ **Santa Barbara:** golden
sand, and not too crowded.

Right: *Not all Corfu's beaches are sandy, but this one at Glifada has rather more than its share.*

Grand and the more modest family-run Glifada Beach. At the moment many of the visitors are day-trippers, and the area is surprisingly quiet in the evenings, with just a handful of tavernas; most people staying nearby eat in one of the two modern hotels. But during the day the beach is in full swing, with every water sport yet invented and with slightly more space on its **broad golden sands** than on the nearby narrower beach of Mirtiotissa. Bathers should take care, as there are known to be strong under-currents just off the shore here. The beach shelves quite deeply in places, so parents should check for safety before allowing children into the water.

Pelekas ★★

Pelekas is one of the few villages behind the coast where tourism has taken off. It is an attractive place, its houses descending in tiers down the wooded hillside, and is famous for the superb **sunset views** over the bay below (where there is a quiet beach, popular with nudists and reached by way of a tricky path down). Pelekas was a favourite place of Kaiser Wilhelm at the turn of the century, when he spent his days at the Achillion Palace. He came over here in the evenings to a spot now known as the **Kaiser's Throne**, an olive-shaded viewpoint at the top of the hill above the town. One of the features that appealed to him was that, at the right time of year, the setting sun can appear to slide down a hillside and into the sea. The views also take in the peak of Mount Pantokrator to the north, as well as both the west and east coasts, including Corfu Town. In Pelekas itself there are small hotels and rooms to rent, bars, shops, tavernas and tourist information offices with car hire available. The village is convenient for the exceptionally good local beaches.

Agios Gordis ★★

This is yet another of Corfu's marvellous, long, west-coast beaches, enclosed by headlands, backed by green hills and rather dominated by a large hotel on the bay. Agios Gordis (there are several variations on its name, including Agios Ghordios or Ai Gordhis) is a beach first and a resort second; quiet in past years, it is now starting to develop, and visitors will find villas going up in the olive groves behind the beach as well as a large **Diving Centre** very evident actually on the beach. Other water sports are available too, and while the beach is a mix of sand and shingle, it shelves gently and therefore appeals to those with young children. There are tavernas and shops nearby, and in summer seven buses daily make the 45-minute journey to Corfu Town, via Sinarades.

Below: *Sunset over Agios Gordis – this is often the most peaceful time of day.*

Sinarades ★

In this sizable hill village between Pelekas and Agios Gordis, two of the traditional houses have been turned into a **Folk Museum** (open Monday–Saturday, 09:00–14:00). It depicts life in a typical 19th-century home, with domestic and agricultural items and a few explanations in German and English. The museum is very low-key, and the more appealing because of it. The village itself is attractive, with flower-bedecked houses and steep, narrow streets.

North of Sinarades is the small, isolated coastal resort of Yaliskari, with a steeply shelving pebbly beach and dominated by the huge Yaliskari Palace Hotel.

Gardiki ★

Gardiki, 10km (6 miles) south of Sinarades, is of greater interest as a historical site than as a tourist attraction – there is little enough to see today. Yet archaeological

finds here have been dated to the Palaeolithic period (about 40,000BC), making it possibly the **oldest settlement** in the Ionian islands. In the comparatively recent 13th century AD, Michael II Angelos Komnenos – the same Despot of Epirus who was responsible for the Angelokastro near Paleokastritsa – built a **fortress** here. There are several higher hills in the area that he might have chosen as more defensible sites, but Gardiki's position was possibly dictated by freshwater springs. Today the fortress lies abandoned and overgrown, but its octagonal outer walls and towers retain their original height.

Not far away is the forest-girt hill village of Agios Mattheos, clinging to the slopes of the mountain from which it takes its name. The summit is crowned by the Pantokrator Monastery, near which is a cave said to have an underground passage leading to the sea far below.

Left: *Not all hotels are high-rise concrete blocks. Some are built bungalow-style, like the one at Kapodistrias pictured here near Moraitika.*
Opposite: *In the interior, quiet roads demand exploration, preferably on foot or by bicycle.*

Messongi ★★

On the east coast, at the point where the busy coastal road turns inland and crosses the Messongi River, there is a sprawl of tourist development in and around the stretch of about 1km (just over half a mile) which separates Messongi from Moraitika. Messongi, where you can still sit in the old village square, has managed to cling on to its original **village atmosphere**, despite the presence nearby of large hotels and a camp site, the construction of villas and the busy nature of the rather ordinary sand and shingle beach. The **waterfront tavernas** are appealing, perfectly situated for patrons to enjoy their mainly fresh fish menus.

The river ensures that the land is well watered, as it has been for centuries: some of the many large **olive trees** in and around the village are said to have been planted up to 700 years ago, when the Venetians first came. Older still are the remains of some ancient Greek temples that have been found, such as one from the 3rd century BC on a hill behind the village. There are pleasant walks to be had by heading inland up the course of the river, and to the south along a coastal track, none of them strenuous as the landscape around here is rather flatter than elsewhere on the island. To explore further afield, there are two bus services to and from Corfu Town, almost hourly in summer.

Moraitika ★

The giant 870-room **Messongi Beach Hotel** is actually on the edge of Moraitika, by the river, and is generally held to mark the 'border' between Messongi and Moraitika. The latter is a fairly scruffy, rambling holiday spot with no heart to it, unless it is the big hotel. There's no lack of other places to stay, including the luxury-class Miramare Beach Hotel, with at least a dozen others from 5-star to 1-star able to accommodate several hundred visitors between them.

The Messongi Beach Hotel is impossible to ignore, with its 10 bars, tavernas, private gardens and shopping centre. Some of its facilities are for residents only, but in the evening it attracts its fair share of non-residents who wine, dine and dance there. The hotel's own strip of beach and the general public beach are both narrow and have shallow waters, ideal for children, if a little cramped in high season. There are all the **water sports** you could wish for – windsurfing, water-skiing, paragliding, boats, canoes, pedaloes – and no shortage of places to eat and drink ranging from genuine Greek tavernas to those catering exclusively to the many British visitors who come here. For evening entertainment there are discos and a wide range of bars. From an earlier more dignified age are the remains of a Greco-Roman villa and bath house, lying just off the main road.

Benitses ★★

Benitses has been a holiday spot since Roman times – the remains of a bath house can be seen near the harbour square – and until recently most visitors behaved as if they were at a Roman orgy. However, the local people tired of this behaviour and in the last few years have tried to make Benitses more of a family resort, with partygoers homing in on Kavos on the south coast.

For all the place's popularity, the beaches are not brilliant and get so crowded in summer that some people resort to sunbathing on the pavements. There are several sections of beach, including a man-made sandy stretch that is popular with families; the rest are small and narrow shingle strips, much frequented by those who are active only at night for the duration of their holiday here. Note, too, that the main road runs straight through Benitses, which can create problems when going to and from the beach. If they are lacking in sand and space, the beaches try to make up for it with their facilities: nowhere

is further than a short stroll from a bar or restaurant, and there is every conceivable water sport. There is also a **go-kart racing track** just outside the town.

Slightly to the north of the town centre and well sign-posted is the **Benitses Shell Museum**. This private collection amassed by the owner over the last 20 years now amounts to several thousand shells, which make for a fascinating display. There are also whale bones and sharks' teeth, snakes and scorpions, and many examples of fine coral in subtle shades. Visitors should note that it is technically illegal to buy and sell coral items, because of the fast-disappearing coral reefs all round the world, but this law is commonly ignored in tourist areas. The shopkeeper might get away with selling you coral, but you could face a fine and confiscation of your purchase if it is found when you are going through customs.

Many people still visit Benitses for the nightlife, not the sea-life, and here the bars and discos stay open until the last customers have gone home. Many offer laser shows, karaoke competitions and other delights but this aspect of Benitses is slowly scaling down so that these days it is lively rather than out of control.

As for accommodation ... the resort has more than 2000 beds in everything from smart 5-star hotels to economic 1-star apartments.

Above: *The colourful harbour at Benitses shows that even the busiest of beach resorts have not lost their Greek look completely.*

HOT FOOD

If you like your food hot, you need to take care what you order and when. Many meals are prepared at lunchtime, and simply kept warm for the evenings, which is how the Greeks like it. Stuffed tomatoes, stuffed peppers, stuffed vine leaves and moussaka are amongst the dishes best eaten at lunchtime, if you prefer to have them hot, while in the evenings you should choose something grilled, which cannot be prepared in advance.

SQUID AND OCTOPUS

Two dishes popular throughout the Mediterranean, but often less so with visitors, are squid and octopus. Fried squid (*kalamaria*) or baby squid (*kalamarakia*) are both popular starters, and delicious if fresh and well-cooked, while octopus (*oktapodhes*) is more often turned into a stew. Octopus meat is tenderized by hurling the creature against a hard surface, such as a rock or the harbour wall – a typical Greek sight.

In among all the holiday activity and nightlife, an ordinary Greek fishing village manages to survive, but the blue and white boats in the harbour are testimony to that, as are the fishermen mending their yellow nets. Inland, too, is evidence of another Corfu, with a lush valley of olive and cypress trees, and **good walking country**. Benitses is only 12km (7¹/₂ miles) from Corfu Town, with buses almost hourly in summer taking 30 minutes to cover the journey to San Rocco Square.

Right: *The back streets of Benitses have their quiet spots, with the buildings regularly whitewashed around the time of Easter every year.*

Mount Agios Deka ★★

Although almost 270m (886ft) lower than Mount Pantokrator, Mount Agios Deka at 576m (1890ft) still dominates this narrow stretch of central Corfu. To reach it by car from Benitses involves a long circular drive round the back of the mountain to the village of Ano Garouna, where the road stops (cars must be left below the village itself), leaving a short walk to the summit. However, if you are reasonably fit a more direct route is to walk from Benitses, a distance of about 3km (2 miles). A track runs alongside the river and heads inland, bringing you to a minor road. If you turn left you reach the hill village of **Stavros**, but a right turn along this road brings you, after about a kilometre, to a track leading off to the left that takes you to the mountain top. If you miss the path you arrive instead at the village of Agios Deka, from where another track heads up to the summit with its **excellent views**.

The Achillion ★★★

Built as a palace and later a casino, it has also seen service as a film set and hospital, been called 'an abomination' and 'monstrous' – and is one of the most visited sights on Corfu. The Achillion Palace was designed by an Italian architect and built in 1890–1 for **Empress Elizabeth of Austria** in a kitsch style that few people other than the empress herself have ever appreciated. She saw it as a retreat from her personal and political problems at the Hapsburg Court, and it has to be said that the view from the Achillion, which stands 150m (492ft) above the coast, is one of its best features – not least because you don't have to look at the palace itself. It has been dubbed neoclassical, neo-Pompeian, Teutonic and a re-creation of a Phaeacian palace, though Lawrence Durrell described it more bluntly as 'a monstrous building'.

One of Durrell's objections was to the ubiquitous sculptures, and it does seem as if you can scarcely turn a corner without bumping into some grand stone representation of a Greek or Roman figure. Principal of these

Below: *The Achillion has had its detractors over the years, but few could deny that it does have its elegant sections.*

ACHILLES

In Greek mythology Achilles was the greatest warrior in the Trojan War, and his deeds are recounted in Homer's *Iliad*. As a child his mother dipped him in the River Styx to make him immortal, but the heel by which she held him did not touch the miraculous water. The *Iliad* opens with Achilles refusing to fight and sulking in his tent, but he is to play a dominant role in the 10-year siege of Troy when roused to anger by the death of his friend Patroklus. He eventually leads the Greek army right to the walls, where he is mortally wounded in his vulnerable heel, an event remembered by us today in the proverbial 'Achilles heel'.

Below: *One statue of Achilles was erected not by Elizabeth but by her successor at the Achillion, Kaiser Wilhelm.*

is **Achilles**, Elizabeth's hero for whom the palace was named and who can be found in various histrionic postures around the place, including one overwhelming carving that is 8m (26ft) high. The grounds and gardens at least are delightful, a green oasis looking down on turquoise seas. It is sad that Elizabeth was unable to enjoy her retreat for long; she was assassinated in 1898 by an Italian anarchist, and nine years later the palace was sold to Kaiser Wilhelm II of Germany. The remains of the 'Kaiser's Bridge' can be seen down on the coast, built jutting out into the sea so that he could step straight off his boat on to land when visiting the palace. The Achillion was used as a hospital during World War I and was the setting for some scenes in the James Bond film *For Your Eyes Only*, an appropriate title given the general opinion of Elizabeth's creation.

Gastouri, the nearest village to the Achillion Palace, is a pleasant antidote to the blatant tourism of the coast and the palace. Tucked in the hills behind Benitses and Perama, it has just a few small hotels and pensions. Coaches headed for the Achillion drive through Gastouri, but it is otherwise untouched by tourism and is noted as a place where traditions in folk music and dancing are strongly maintained. It also claims to have the most beautiful women on the island, who wear their hair piled high up on their heads in a manner unique to the village.

Perama ★

On the opposite side of the Halikiopoulos Lagoon from Mouse Island and connected to Kanoni by a causeway, Perama is the first major resort to the south of Corfu Town. It shares with Kanoni the problem of being very **close to the airport** with planes coming in to land over the causeway. This does not appear to have hindered Perama's development as a holiday destination, however; perhaps visitors agree with the local guide, who – transforming the problem into an asset – declares that Perama 'is a good place to watch the planes landing and taking off from the nearby airport'.

Perama is a sprawling place, which has grown out from a small, once-attractive centre, where the Durrell family first lived when they arrived on Corfu. The finding of, and the nerve-racking drive to the 'Strawberry-Pink' villa is hilariously described in an early chapter of Gerald Durrell's *My Family and Other Animals*, an essential read for anyone interested in discovering what Perama was like only 60 years ago. Today, hotels line the main southern coastal road. There are several beaches although they are mostly small and of shingle: the resorts on this coast cannot compete with those on the west, with their sweeping sandy bays. However, between them, Perama's beaches cover most water sports options, such as paragliding, water-skiing and the usual canoes, pedaloes and boat hire.

While there is no shortage of bars, restaurants and shopping facilities, Perama, with just two late-night discos, cannot compete with nearby Benitses when it comes to nightlife. Benitses is only 3.5km (2 miles) away, and Corfu Town itself not much further in the other direction. In summer there is an almost hourly bus service linking Perama with Benitses and the capital. The resort's main appeal lies in the fact that it has an attractive green, wooded backdrop, a lushness which harks back to the times of the *Odyssey* for this is yet another spot with a Homeric connection, as it is claimed that the luxuriant gardens of the Phaeacian King Alcinous were to be found here.

THE SOUTH
Agios Yioryios ★★

Not to be confused with the several other similarly named villages scattered around Corfu, this Agios Yioryios is another **thriving beach resort**. On the west coast, it is a multi-beach resort with a pair of wide, long, sandy stretches either side of a rocky outcrop, and many other beaches outside the village itself. In all, the beaches stretch for almost 12km (7$\frac{1}{2}$ miles), to the far end of Lake Korission in the north and south past developing resorts such as Agia Varvara, generally known as Santa Barbara,

---

TRADITIONAL DRESS

You are unlikely to see traditional costumes being worn today other than on special occasions and at folk dancing displays. The male costume is fairly standard, featuring black pantaloons and jacket over white shirt and long white stockings, but there are four types of female costume, each named after a different region of the island: *orous* (from the mountains) *agrou* (from the plains), *mesi* (from the centre) and *Lefkimi* (from the Lefkimi region). Unfortunately there is no substantial collection of costumes for visitors to see – just a few in the Sinarades Folk Museum.

BEST BARS

Bars change hands regularly in a busy tourist area like Corfu, so recommendations are difficult to give. Check the local monthly English-language publications such as *The Corfiot* and *Liston*, which carry advertisements as well as write-ups on what is happening. Look for **'Happy Hours'** as a cheaper way of trying out a new bar and check prices before you buy.

to a small cape called **Megakhoros**. One stretch to the south is known as Golden Beach, narrow and shelving steeply – and immensely popular. There are so many beaches along this part of the coast that it should always be possible to find space to yourself if that is your wish; certain sections are used as unofficial nudist beaches.

As a place, Agios Yioryios has little heart or soul to it, having been built up purely to cater to the tourist trade; it certainly fulfils that function being noted for good swimming and with a wealth of **water sports** – water-skiing, diving, windsurfing, boating and so on. There are several small hotels, though as yet no huge ones, with much of the accommodation in apartments and small self-catering villas. Car hire is available, and is recommended if you want to explore more than the beaches, as there is only one bus a day making the hour-long trip to Corfu Town, or to Paleokastritsa.

Santa Barbara ★

Long undiscovered, though now on the map, Santa Barbara (Agia Varvara) is a quieter spot than its neighbour to the west, Agios Yioryios. At present it consists of little more than a deep golden, sandy beach with a few tavernas and good windsurfing conditions – there is no village as such. But facilities are increasing: already there are rooms to rent, a few small shops and evidence of more building work to. This strip is also known as Maltas or Marathias, the names of two neighbouring beaches.

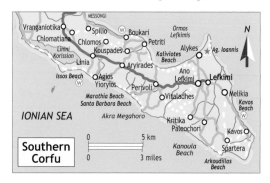

Ionian Sea

Left: *Sunset at the southern village of Agios Yioryios, when the smell of fish grilling on charcoal starts to draw the crowds to the tavernas.*

Lake Korission ★★

This large, shallow lake in southwest Corfu is not only excellent for sunbathing, with miles of sands and dunes, it also harbours a wealth of wildlife. You don't even need to be a keen walker to observe the wildlife: there is access for cars right to the edge of the lake. Many wading birds take advantage of the expanse of fresh water, which is a rarity on Corfu. You should see common waders such as sandpipers, dunlin, avocets and greenshanks, and – if you're lucky – catch a glimpse of great egrets and glossy ibis. In season the wild duck attract Greek hunters. Local wild flowers include Jersey orchids in spring and sea daffodils on the dunes in autumn.

Petriti ★★

Petriti is the largest of a clutch of villages clustered together along a stretch of the east coast on Lefkimi Bay. They have some tourist facilities but are in no way developed to the extent of Kavos and Agios Yioryios. In Petriti you are likely to be searching for something to

TOUCHING BEHAVIOUR

The Greeks are tactile people. Babies are cuddled, children have their hair ruffled, men often greet each other with a pat or a hug, and elderly people can be seen walking hand in hand with their grandchildren in the street. Young girls hold hands, and male friends may walk arm in arm. While this is normally restricted to friends and relatives, visitors may also be subject to such touches, which is a natural part of Greek behaviour. Women on their own, of course, need to keep alert and be watchful for the point where friendly touching may start to turn into unwelcome physical attention.

do in the evening rather than being spoilt for choice. There are a few tavernas, one bar, some shops and no beach facilities. In fact the beach here is just a small stretch of pebbles, but you will find no shortage of sandy beaches if you take a short walk either north or south. There is one hotel and several places offer rooms to rent. **Boukari**, a similar but even tinier village around the headland to the north of Petriti, has two small 20-room hotels. Either Petriti or Boukari will appeal to anyone who wishes to have a peaceful holiday in a traditional fishing village.

Kavos ★★

It seems incongruous to find Kavos right at the southern end of Corfu, literally the last resort before Cape Asprokavos, the island's southernmost point, marked by a derelict monastery. With quiet bays, fishing villages and agricultural settlements all around, suddenly Kavos explodes like a firework. It does have one of the best beaches at this end of the island, a long stretch of sand that runs for 3km (2 miles) with a view across the Ionian

Right: *Kavos is quite a large community in the sparsely populated south, with most people to be found on its justifiably popular beach.*

Left: *While most visitors worry about their tans, this Kavos fisherman makes sure his nets are ready for his next trip out to sea.*

Sea to the mainland. It also shelves slowly, making it ideal for young children, but any children brought here would need to be sound sleepers, for Kavos is the kind of place where the **bars and discos** stay open until the sun comes up or their customers fall down. There are said to be over 100 bars and clubs here and, though not quite so many restaurants, certainly no shortage of choice, with good seafood restaurants on the waterfront.

Every beach facility and water sport has been thought of: you can have sunbeds, umbrellas, canoes, pedaloes, water-skiing, paragliding and windsurfing, and boat trips south to the island of Paxos or north along the coast to Corfu Town. The bus to the capital takes almost two hours, but there is a good regular service. There are no really large hotels, most of the accommodation being in villas and blocks of self-catering apartments which are pre-booked for the season by the many tour companies, mostly British, which sell packaged holidays to Kavos (it is a popular destination for British under-thirties). It's certainly not for everyone, but if you're looking for an outrageous time, Kavos will not disappoint you.

SWEET HARMONIES

In addition to brass bands and more traditional Greek music, Corfu has a long tradition of classical music too, with no less than 15 orchestras on the island. The **Philharmonic Society** was formed in 1840 by the Corfiot musician, Nikolaos Mantzaros, who subsequently provided the music for the Greek national anthem. The Olympic Anthem was also composed by a member of the society, and performed by its orchestra at the first modern Olympic Games in Athens in 1896.

Central and South Corfu at a Glance

In **midsummer –** if you like it hot and busy – the main resorts are at their peak then; in **spring** or **autumn** for peace and warm weather. If you're keen on **folklore**, Lefkimi (the south's administrative centre) holds an annual folk festival and fiesta on 8 July.

There are a number of services from Corfu Town's various **bus** stations to Ermones, Benitses, Glifada, Messongi, Perama and Vatos, and a good regular bus service runs from the New Fortress bus station to Kavos, via Messongi and the south's inland villages of Aryirades, Perivoli and Lefkimi. The closer coastal resorts are easily reachable by **taxi** from the airport. You can **rent a car** on arrival in Corfu Town – there are well known international companies such as Avis and Hertz here as well as local firms. Moped hire is not recommended: many visitors have been involved in accidents because of poor road surfaces and unsatisfactorily maintained machines.

In addition to the bus services, the coast road makes **taxis** a quick option for the east-coast resorts in central Corfu, with **boat** excursions and **hitch-hiking** being other easy alternatives. In the south, use the frequent bus service along the solitary main road down the centre. From the road,

nowhere is much more than 3km (2 miles) distant. Taxis are also a reasonable option, with **boats** from the main resorts serving some of the more remote beaches. **Car hire** is an alternative if you want to feel independent. Most resorts have car rental offices.

Agios Gordis
Agios Gordios, tel: 26610 53320–2. The main 4-star hotel in this resort, standing on its own at the end of the bay, with garden and sea views. Small swimming pool; beach is reached down a steep slope. **Alonakia**, tel: 26610 53102–4, website: www.alonakiahotel.gr 3-star pension with 30 rooms.

Agios Yioryios
Hotel Golden Sands, tel: 26620 51225. Medium-sized, family-owned 3-star hotel with pool, playground, bar, restaurant and nearby beach. Entertainment includes live music and barbecues.

Benitses
Regency, tel: 26610 71211–8. 4-star; away from the resort centre, with pool, poolside bar, children's pool, sauna, disco. **San Stefano**, tel: 26610 71117, fax: 72272. 4-star hotel set in 14ha (34 acres) of olive groves. **Achilles**, tel: 26610 72425, website: www.achilles-corfu.com Medium-sized 3-star hotel well out of the centre with its own beach (pebbly), sun terraces and garden.

Potamaki, tel: 26610 72201 / 71140. Large 3-star in the centre of the resort, convenient for shops and bus to Corfu Town. **Le Mirage**, tel: 26610 72062. Small apartment-style 2-star hotel in the centre of the resort but off the main road.

Boukari
Boukari Beach, tel: 26620 51791, website: www.boukaribeach.gr Lovely family-run villas in the unspoilt little beach village of Boukari.

Ermones
Philoxenia, tel: 26610 94660, website: www.hotelphiloxenia.gr Delightful new 3-star hotel, 100m from the beach. 50 spacious rooms all have balconies and there's a pool, children's pool and a playroom. **Athena Ermones Golf**, tel: 26610 94226. Small 2-star in a secluded position, 5 minutes' walk from sandy beach.

Glifada
Louis Grand Hotel Glifada, tel: 26610 94201 or 94140–5, website: www.louishotels.com A 4-star establishment with 247 rooms, sports, water sports, shopping, bars, restaurant and most other facilities. **Glifada Beach**, tel: 26610 94257–8. Medium-sized 2-star; 5 minutes from the beach.

Kavos
Hotel Morfeas, tel: 26620 61300–2. 2-star hotel with rooftop restaurant and a party atmosphere.

Central and South Corfu at a Glance

Messongi
Gemini, tel: 26610 75211–2.
The best in the place, a 3-star
hotel on the main square,
with pool and restaurant.

Moraitika
Miramare Beach, tel: 26610
75224. 5-star hotel with its
own beach, gardens and
shopping facilities.
Messongi Beach Hotel,
tel: 26610 75830, website:
www.messonghibeach.gr
Vast 3-star hotel with every
facility and 870 rooms spread
over several buildings within
large grounds.
Delifinia, tel: 26610 76320,
website: www.delfiniahotels.gr
A complex of three large modern buildings with two pools,
tennis and all the water sports,
restaurants and bars. Lots of
children's activities too.

Perama
Alexandros, tel: 26610
36855–7. The only 5-star
hotel in this sprawling resort,
situated right in the centre.
Aeolos Beach, tel: 26610
33133–6, website: www.
aeolosbeach.gr 3-star hotel
set above the coast road 15
minutes' walk from the resort;
has its own beach, gardens, a
pool, playground and disco.
Oasis, tel: 26610 33120 /
38190, website: www.corfu
oasis.com Medium-sized 3-star
hotel in the resort centre with
its own beach and gardens.
Pontikonissi, tel: 26610
36871 / 45412–4. 2-star hotel
on the coast road, about 10

minutes' walk from the centre, with own small beach.
Nicely designed in terraces,
but suffers from aircraft noise.

WHERE TO EAT

Benitses
Mythos Grill Room, tel:
26610 72050. Right by the
little park near the entrance
into Old Benitses, the Mythos
serves real Greek food such as
the local special of *pastitsáda*.

Kavos
Pavlos, is a popular restaurant,
though there is little really to
choose between the several
lively eating places offering
similar menus, such as
Petros or **Krinos**.

Messongi
Almond Tree, this restaurant
boasts a lovely beachside
setting, with barbecues and
fresh fish.
Galini Restaurant, right on
the beach with a mix of
English and Greek cuisine.

Moraitika
The Valentino, unpromising
setting but has a wide menu
typical of such resorts covering Greek, Chinese, British
and French cooking.

Pelekas
Sunset Restaurant, the place
above town to emulate the
Kaiser and watch the sun go
down; you pay for the privilege.
In the village there are simple
tavernas that serve local dishes.
Try the **Acropolis** or **Panorama**.

Perama
The Pierotto, not surprisingly
this restaurant is very popular,
as much for its view across to
Mouse Island as for its Greek
cuisine.

Santa Barbara
Dionysos, restaurant and bar
offering a mix of Greek and
Italian cooking.

Vatos
**Olympic Restaurant and
Grill**, can be recommended,
which is just as well as it is
the only choice.

TOURS AND EXCURSIONS

Sinarades Travel at
Agios Gordis, tel: 26610
53036 / 53643, website:
www.sinaradestravel.com
e-mail: sinntrvl@otenet.gr
Can arrange your accommo-
dation, car and boat hire,
plane and boat tickets.

USEFUL CONTACTS

The Achillion,
tel: 26610 56245.
Benitses Shell Museum,
tel: 26610 72227.
Calypso Diving Centre,
Agios Gordis,
tel: 26610 53101.
Kostas Jet Ski, (no phone) is at
the northern end of the beach
at Agios Yioryios, with safety
skiing for children and boats
to rent.
**Mesongi Beach Hotel
Diving Centre**,
tel: 26610 83295.
Sinarades Folk Museum,
tel: 26610 54962 / 49084.

6
Excursions

Corfu is well placed for venturing further afield. No matter where you are based, you will easily be able to get to other nearby Ionian islands and even across to the mainland. Even if there are no direct trips from your base, few villages are so remote as not to have a bus service to Corfu Town, which opens up numerous options. Be adventurous and you will discover peaceful worlds far removed from the sometimes frenetic beach and bar life of Corfu itself.

Paxi (Paxos) and Antipaxi (Antipaxos) ★★★

It is only 11km (7 miles) from southern Corfu to the smaller island of **Paxi**. Trips can be booked in most resorts. Only 2500 people live on Paxi, which measures just 10km by 4km (6 miles by 2¹/₂ miles), most in the main town and port, Gaios. Apart from tourism, the island's industries are fishing and olive growing: olive oil is a good buy, being of very high quality.

Gaios is in a lovely setting, its white houses gathered around a harbour and half-hidden from the sea by a large tree-covered island in the bay. It is a lively harbour town, made busy by visiting yachts and the countless day-trippers from Corfu and the mainland resorts, but it is still very much a working waterfront town, typical of hundreds throughout Greece. Fish tavernas are plentiful, and good beaches only a short walk away. There is only one hotel, but plenty of rooms to rent in Gaios.

Antipaxi is smaller still, making Paxi look cosmopolitan, and there is no accommodation unless you can

---

FERRY CONFUSING

The Ionian Islands are linked by a complicated ferry network. Timetables change annually, so get a current timetable from the **NTOG**. One thing to note is that many tourist offices act as agents for only one of the several ferry lines. If you wish to travel on, say, a Tuesday, when a rival company operates, the office will deny the existence of that ferry and try to persuade you to book on their own next available service. Try several agencies, or contact the port authorities.

Opposite: *Antipaxi is still unspoilt and only a short boat ride from Corfu.*

PAXI FESTIVALS

The most important date in the year is **29 June**, the feast of St Peter and St Paul, when a procession takes place in the saints' honour. It visits their church, as well as the Church of the Holy Apostles and the tomb of St Gaius, who gave his name to the island's capital, Gaios. He has his own feast day on **5 November**. On the tiny islet of Panayia in Gaios harbour, **15 August** is an important day, with a daytime pilgrimage to the monastery there. In the evening the feast continues in the main square on Gaios with visitors not just welcomed but encouraged.

rent a room in someone's house. Only 120 people inhabit the island all year round, living mostly off their vineyards, fruit and fishing. Boats cross regularly from Gaios, and will drop visitors at one or another of the island's numerous beautiful sandy beaches, many of which have tavernas open in season.

THE OTHER IONIAN ISLANDS

The other four main islands in the Ionian group – Lefkada, Ithaka, Kefalonia and Zakynthos – lie close

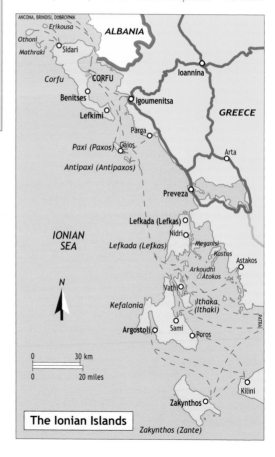

The Ionian Islands

together, with Corfu about 60km (37 miles) to the north. Because of the distances involved, day trips are not feasible, but connections are quite good if you are prepared to stay for a night or two. Contact one of the tourist offices for ferry details. Services are obviously more frequent in

summer and there are regular flights between several of the Ionian islands.

Above: *Zakynthos Town was rebuilt after an earthquake in 1953, but retains much of its charm.*

Lefkada (Lefkas) ★

Hardly an island at all, Lefkada is connected to the Greek mainland by a causeway. It is an attractive, green place, where many women still wear traditional dress, and has been the slowest of the Ionian islands to develop for tourism, although that is now changing. The coast is proving very popular with windsurfers, in particular the small resorts of **Nidhri** and **Vassiliki**, but inland there are many unspoilt rural villages, making Lefkada a great island for those who enjoy exploring off the beaten track. **Lefkada Town** has most of the accommodation on the island, but no beach. Similarly, the handful of villages with rooms to rent tend to be some distance from a beach. This is not a problem if you don't mind a walk, as there are numerous good sandy beaches around.

Kefalonia ★★★

Mountainous Kefalonia is larger than Corfu, and while parts of it have been given over very much to tourism, its size means that there are still quiet beach resorts, hill villages and deserted sandy coves. The fishing village of **Fiskardo** is a rarity here in that its 18th-century Venetian houses remained in act after the devastating 1953 earthquake that destroyed almost every other community on Kefalonia (and on Zakynthos). The area around **Mount Enos** (1632m; 5355ft), the highest point in the Ionian

> ### LOVER'S LEAP
>
> **Lefkada** can claim the original Lover's Leap, at Cape Doukata at the extreme southern tip of the island. The poet **Sappho** was allegedly the first to take the plunge over the 60m (200ft) white cliffs in the name of unrequited love, a practice continued in later years by lovelorn Roman youths, the gesture somewhat spoiled by the fact that they often strapped birds to themselves in the hope that they might fly.

islands, is a national park, created to protect the fir trees after which the island is named: *Abies cephalonica*. Also protected are the loggerhead turtles who have one of their main nesting sites here. There are plenty of hotels on the island.

Ithaka (Ithaki) ★★

Renowned as the home island of **Odysseus**, rocky Ithaka is a great place to get away from it all by relaxing and visiting the sites associated with Homer's hero. Not that there is any historical proof of their authenticity, but the stories *could* be true – and local guides will convince you that they are. The port and main town, **Vathi**, has a few small hotels and rooms to rent, but the island lacks good beaches.

Zakynthos (Zante) ★★★

This island could hardly be more different from Ithaka. It has dozens of sweeping sandy beaches and sees a tourist invasion every summer, although the island is large enough to appeal equally to those who like to get away from the crowds. Most visitors flock to the beach resorts around **Laganas** in the south, a bay that runs for 14km (9 miles). Unfortunately this is a traditional nesting site for loggerhead turtles and efforts have been made to ensure that both visitors and turtles can manage to co-exist. Elsewhere are smaller resorts such as **Alykes** in the north, a string of mountain villages and – a popular attraction – the **Fianou Caves** (or Blue Grotto) on Zakynthos' northern tip. Here the waters seemingly turn bathers blue; a boat trip into the Grotto is delightful.

To the Greek Mainland

Just a short boat journey away from Corfu is the coast of **Epirus**, with two main destinations: Parga and Igoumenitsa.

Parga ★★

This is a busy and appealing seaside resort, much like many on Corfu though it has the additional charm of picturesque back streets with white houses covered in tumbling bougainvillaea and bright hibiscus. The beach is first class, with others nearby, and a day trip that allows time to visit the castle and dine at the seafront tavernas is an attractive outing from Corfu.

Igoumenitsa ★

By contrast with Parga, this is a dull seaport, whose only attraction to most people will be as a means of getting to the other Ionian islands, or out into Epirus to explore the nearby mainland for a day or two.

Ioannina ★★★

Ioannina, situated about 50km (31 miles) from Igoumenitsa, is the capital of the Epirus region. It is a busy town but with much to offer the visitor. Here Ali Pasha (*see* panel, page 18) had his court, and his impressive castle can be visited. Ioannina stands on a lake, in the middle of which is **Nissi** (meaning 'island') where, in the Monastery of Pendelimonos, Ali Pasha was killed in 1822. The bullet holes in the floorboards can still be seen.

On the edge of Ioannina are the **Perama Caves**, the largest cave network in Greece, with guided tours throughout the year and well worth seeing. Not to be missed is a visit to the historical site of **Dodona**, 22km (14 miles) away at the end of a winding road into the hills. The theatre here is almost 2300 years old, but the site is even older and better known as the place where the Oracle of Zeus could be consulted.

Dolphins in Danger

The sight of dolphins in the seas off Corfu is not uncommon. They are most easily seen when the surface is calm, making them more visible when they break the surface. The ease with which they can be spotted belies the true picture, which is that their numbers are being reduced for various reasons. One is pollution, another the fact that they are often trapped in fishing nets. The visitor can only try to avoid adding to the pollution, and express concern for their welfare to local people if the opportunity arises.

Below: *On the coast of Epirus, opposite Corfu, Parga is the most attractive of several resorts in the area.*

Right: *There are no ancient theatres on Corfu, but this one at Dodona near Ioannina is one of the best in the whole of Greece.*

Albania ★★★

Daytrips to Albania are possible from Corfu Town and many of the holiday resorts around the island. Ask at any travel agent for further details of day trips and overnight stays too. It takes about 40 minutes to cross from Corfu Town to the Albanian port of **Saranda**, from where there are optional additional excursions to see some of Albania's fine Roman remains.

FURTHER AFIELD

From Ioannina you could head north to the Pindus Mountains and the dramatic **Vikos Gorge**, the second-longest gorge in Europe after Crete's Samaria Gorge, but much more rugged and remote. The gorge is surrounded by the fascinating **Zagorian villages** (*see* panel, this page).

East of Ioannina is the traditional mountain village of **Metsovo**, and beyond that the unique hilltop monasteries of the **Meteora** perched atop the weird rock formations which jut out of the Plain of Thessaly. Further east still is the home of the Gods, **Mount Olympus**, which at 2917m (9570ft) is the highest mountain in Greece. South from Ioannina spectacular roads lead through the hills of northern Greece to the Gulf of Corinth and the **Peloponnese**, a large, relatively non-commercial region occupying the most southern part of Greece.

ZAGORIAN VILLAGES

The Zagorian villages – 46 of them – that cluster round the Vikos Gorge north of Ioannina have a very distinctive look. Narrow cobbled lanes meander between stone houses, many of them formerly grand mansions built with money remitted by Zagorian men forced to seek work away from their poor and remote homeland. The villages are linked by ancient footpaths, taken across rivers by sturdy packhorse bridges. Some of the villages are now crumbling, others are inhabited by just a few families, while the more accessible flourish, many boasting one small hotel and basic tourist facilities.

Excursions at a Glance

There can be pressure on accommodation in July and August, and no accommodation to be had in out-of-the-way places from November to Easter, so **May–June** and **September–October** are ideal, both practically and for the weather.

There are hourly **ferries** between Corfu Town and Igoumenitsa, and several ferries a week that go from Corfu Town to Paxi, Ithaka, Kefalonia and to Patras in the Peloponnese. In season these are augmented by other services, such as hydrofoils between Corfu Town, Lefkada, Ithaka, Paxi, Kefalonia and Preveza on the mainland. In addition there are daytrips to Parga, Paxi and Antipaxi. The other Ionian islands are mostly linked to one another by direct ferries, which also connect with the mainland.

Car hire is available in all the ports listed, except for Paxi and Antipaxi, where cars are less necessary. In midsummer it would be advisable to book ahead through the nearest tourist office. Bicycles, mopeds and motorcycles can be hired on all the islands. The larger islands have good bus services, as do the mainland ports, both local and long-distance, linking them with Athens.

Kefalonia
White Rocks Hotel and Bungalows, tel: 26710 28332, website: www.whiterocks.gr Unashamed luxury on the edge of Argostoli with 102 rooms and 60 bungalows in beautiful gardens.
Ioannina
Kastro, tel: 26510 82866, Great location inside castle.
Ithaka (Ithaki)
Omirikon Hotel, Vathi, tel: 26740 33596, website: www.omirikonhotel.com Stylish hotel on a quiet part of Vathi harbour.
Lefkada (Lefkas)
Ionian Blue Hotel and Spa, tel: 26450 29029. Luxury hotel with eye-catching decor near Nikiana on the east coast.
Parga
Valtos Beach and Gogozotos Residence, tel: 26840 31005, website: www.valtosbeach.gr Highly recommended, by the beach just outside the centre of Parga.
Paxi (Paxos)
Paxos Beach, Gaios, tel: 26620 31211, website: www.paxosbeachhotel.gr One of the best on the island; 3-star with many facilities.
Zagorian Villages
Hotel Gouris, tel: 26530 81214. In the mountain town of Tsepelovo; a good base.
Zakynthos (Zante)
Strada Marina, tel: 26950 42761–3, website: www.stradamarina.gr Convenient large 3-star hotel near the port.

Kefalonia
Captains Cabin, Fiskardo, tel: 26740 41007. Long-established favourite, cooking up family recipes on the harbour.
Ithaka (Ithaki)
Liberty, Vathi, tel: 26740 32561. Smart new place with superb and stylish food, reflecting Ithaka's up-market move.
Lefkada (Lefkas)
Regantos, on main square of Lefkada Town; traditional taverna serving local specialities.
Parga
Oskar, very popular Greek-Italian place with good pizzas as well as Greek favourites.
Paxi (Paxos)
Taverna Nassos, excellent home-cooked food on the harbour in Loggos.
Zakynthos (Zante)
Mantalena, near Alykes; some of the island's best home-cooked food.

Excursions can be booked at any number of tourist offices, and you are unlikely to find any variation in price by shopping around, though you may find some offices offering a wider choice of options.
Corfu Town
Tours to Albania can be arranged through **Sipa Tours** (tel: 26610 56415, website: www.sipatours.com) run by a charming Albanian now living in Corfu. For cruises to the mainland and other islands, see the **Sarris Company**, at Venizelou 13, tel: 26610 25317.

Travel Tips

Tourist Information
The Greek National Tourist Organization (NTOG)
currently has no office in Corfu Town, so if you are in need of information ask around on your visit to see if a new office has opened up. There are also small tourist information centres, such as kiosks in **San Rocco Square** and on the **Esplanade**. There are private 'Tourist Offices' in every resort, and these sell boat tickets, rent out cars, and offer excursions and other services such as restaurant bookings and transport. Most will happily give general advice without charge. There are NTOG offices in:

Australia
37–49 Pitt Street,
Sydney, NSW 2000,
tel: 029241 1663,
fax: 029235 2499.

Canada
1500 Don Mills Road,
Suite 102, Toronto, Ontario
M3B 3K4, tel: 416 968 2220,
fax: 416 968 6533.

UK
4 Conduit Street, London
W1R 0DJ, tel: 020 7495
9300, fax: 020 7495 4057.

USA
645 Fifth Avenue,
New York, NY 10022,
tel: 212 421 5777,
fax: 212 826 6940.

Entry Documents
If you are visiting for less than three months, a passport valid for the whole period of your stay is all that is required for EU citizens and for most other countries too. Longer stays require a **visa**, so contact the Tourist Police or NTOG if this proves necessary. Some nationalities may require visas, so check if you are uncertain. You may be refused entry to Greece if your passport bears a stamp from northern (Turkish-occupied) Cyprus.

Customs
The amounts of wine, spirits, tobacco, cigars, cigarettes and other goods that can be taken into and out of Corfu vary enormously depending on whether you are travelling to or from an EU country, a non-EU European country or a country outside Europe, and also according to whether the

goods were bought duty-free or duty-paid. Visitors should check in their country of residence before travelling. Antiquities and works of art pre-1830 cannot be exported from Greece without permission, such permission being rare. The importation of some prescription drugs is illegal without supporting medical documentation, and **codeine** cannot be imported. There is no limit on the import or export of foreign currency in euros, or of traveller's cheques. However, if bringing into the country over $10,000 or its equivalent, you must declare this on arrival.

Health Requirements
No vaccination certificates are required if visiting Corfu, unless you have recently been to a country where **yellow fever** or **cholera** are prevalent.

Air Travel
Corfu has one **airport**, on the southern outskirts of Corfu Town. A courtesy coach meets Olympic Airways scheduled flights and takes

passengers to the airline's office in Polila (where you can also pick up a coach for your return flight). There is a taxi rank directly outside the terminal. As happens universally, journeys to and from the airport are frequently overcharged, so insist that the taxi meter is switched on. The fare from the airport to Corfu Town should be about €10. If in doubt, ask for a receipt with a note of the driver's number and take the matter up with the Tourist Police.

There are a few direct scheduled flights to Corfu from some European cities, and dozens of direct charter flights from Europe every week in summer. At other times, flights to Corfu will require a change in Athens and a domestic flight with Olympic Airways. The flight from Athens to Corfu takes about one hour, and there is a daily service, although winter flights may be cancelled if the plane is not sufficiently full. Always **reconfirm** your reservation two to three days before departure.

Road Travel

Corfu has a good road network and, being a small island, can be largely covered in a few days. Take care driving on mountain roads, watching out for rough surfaces, blind bends and wandering animals. Corfu Town is best avoided, as the streets can be chaotic, some are pedestrianized, parking is

difficult and a one-way system operates which can suddenly take you out of your way. A knowledge of the **Greek alphabet** is helpful if travelling off the main roads, although all the major resorts have road signs in both Greek and English. **Hitch-hiking** is not usually a problem in Greece. Drivers stop fairly readily, and any reluctance is mainly due to the fact that most Greek motor insurance does not cover the driver for damage to passengers.

Driver's Licence: Theoretically an International Driver's Licence is required if driving in Greece or when renting a car, but in practice only a valid driver's licence will be requested, unless yours happens to be in a particularly obscure language.

Road Rules: Greek drivers ignore most of these, so the visiting driver should be doubly cautious. This is not a facetious comment: Greece has one of the worst **accident rates** in Europe. Maintain a safe distance between yourself and any driver in front, and keep well in to the side when going round bends as Greeks like to drive down the middle of the road. Officially they drive on the right, and should give priority to traffic coming from the right unless otherwise indicated. **Seat belts** are compulsory and it is forbidden to sound your horn in built-up areas. You must also carry a warning triangle, a fire extinguisher and a first aid kit.

Speed Limits: 50kph (31mph) in built-up areas, 80kph (49mph) outside these and 100kph (62mph) on motorways and dual carriageways.

Fuel: Unleaded petrol is widely available, and petrol stations are plentiful, though they may be closed on Sundays and during the afternoon.

Car Hire: There are numerous car rental firms in Corfu Town, including the major international names. Several of these also have offices at the airport and many have agencies in the major resorts. A reputable name may be more expensive, but the car is likely to be more regularly checked. Agreements can be for limited or unlimited mileage, so be sure you know what you are getting. Also check the **insurance cover** carefully, as some policies do not cover damage to third parties. Be sure you have Collision Damage Waiver insurance.

Maps

Good road maps in most of the major European languages are widely available in Corfu, and almost all include a street plan of Corfu Town. If planning to drive to out-of-the-way places, it might be useful to choose a map which also shows place names in Greek.

Clothes: What to Pack

If travelling between June and September, **travel light**. Corfu is informal as well as warm, and very few places require formal dress. Take a sweater for the occasional cool evening, and an umbrella in the spring and autumn. Both men and women should have some means of covering up slightly if planning to visit a monastery, otherwise shorts, T-shirts and casual wear is all that is needed.

Money Matters

The Greek currency is the euro (EUR or €) and there are coins for 1 and 2 euros as well as 1, 2, 5, 10, 20 and 50 cents. Notes are for 5, 10, 20, 50, 100 and 500 euros.

Currency Exchange: You can change foreign currency or travellers' cheques at banks, bureaux de change and at many hotels and tourist offices. There are dozens of such places in Corfu Town, including American Express and Thomas Cook. Travellers' cheques can often be used to pay bills in hotels and some restaurants.

Banks: There are no banks outside Corfu Town, but bank buses tour the island. Opening hours are normally 08:30–14:00 from Monday to Friday only, although in season some may open in the evenings and on weekend mornings for currency exchanges. A separate window is usually used, so look for the 'Exchange' sign. You will need your passport to change travellers' cheques but not for currency.

Credit Cards: Some large shops, restaurants, car hire firms and hotels accept major international credit cards, but many smaller ones do not, so don't assume that you can survive in Corfu on plastic money only. Always have some currency or travellers' cheques. There are many cash machines that give cash on visa and access cards. You must know your pin since only the National bank will give cash inside the bank and this process takes hours.

Sales Tax: Prices in restaurants are in two columns, without and with tax: the customer must pay the higher price. Otherwise, the price you see is the price you pay, although tourists will inevitably pay more for a drink than local customers.

Tipping: Tipping is informal throughout Greece. The usual practice in restaurants or with taxi drivers is to tell them to keep the change. Add a little if you feel you have had very good service. In tavernas, it is common to leave a tip of a few euros for the young boy employed to serve wine and clear tables. In hotels, a small tip for porters and for chambermaids at the end of your stay is not expected but will be appreciated.

Accommodation

Accommodation is graded by the Tourist Police from 5-star through to 1-star establishments, which provides a fair guide to standards but is not infallible. Facilities such as telephones in the rooms with count for more than the fact that the room is rather dingy. Corfu has several 5-star hotels, which are of the standard you would expect internationally from such a grade. There are 4-star hotels in most of the major resorts. Both the 4-star and 3-star hotels will generally have all or most rooms with private facilities, some with telephones and televisions. 2-star would normally lack private facilities, but usually be clean, whereas 1-star are very much the budget choices. Apartments are also checked by the Tourist Police.

CONVERSION CHART

From	To	Multiply By
Millimetres	Inches	0.0394
Metres	Yards	1.0936
Metres	Feet	3.281
Kilometres	Miles	0.6214
Square kilometres	Square miles	0.386
Hectares	Acres	2.471
Litres	Pints	1.760
Kilograms	Pounds	2.205
Tonnes	Tons	0.984

To convert Celsius to Fahrenheit: x 9 ÷ 5 + 32

An official notice of the grade and the room price (based on a Tourist Police inspection) should be displayed in the room – it's usually to be found on the back of the door. This can be slightly out of date, if the current year's inspection has not yet been carried out. A small variation in price can usually be safely ignored; if in doubt, check with the hotel management. Suspicion of gross overcharging should be reported to the Tourist Police. Breakfast is not usually included in the room price, leaving you the option of eating in or going to a local café. '**Rooms to rent**' signs are common outside houses in resorts. These may be self-catering apartments or simply the use of a room in someone's house, sharing facilities with the family. These can be delightful or dreadful, so approach them with an open mind. The signs may also read 'Zimmer' or 'Domatia'.

Plumbing

Greek plumbing uses small-bore pipes, which easily become blocked by toilet paper. Only in newer hotels will it be safe to flush paper down the toilet. Elsewhere, bins are provided in bathrooms for the disposal of toilet paper. This may seem unhygienic, but is less unpleasant than a blocked toilet.

Trading Hours

Shops normally open Monday to Saturday from 08:00 to 13:00, then close for the afternoon, reopening at about 17:00 until 20:00. Souvenir shops and others in tourist areas may stay open later, and some may stay open in the afternoon, but supermarkets and general stores will normally close. Non-tourist shops will also usually close on a public holiday and on a feast day. Some close on the eve of important feasts too, and may not open on the day after, depending on how well the celebrations went.

Public Holidays

These are 1 January, 6 January, First Day of Lent (Clean Monday), 25 March, Good Friday, Easter Monday, Whit Monday, 1 May, 15 August, 28 October and 25/26 December.
Half holidays, when shops close in the mornings, are on

BOOKS TO BRING

Apart from the inevitable books by Lawrence and Gerald Durrell, Henry Miller's *The Colosssus of Maroussi* contains an entertaining account of the American writer's first visit to Corfu. *A Kitchen in Corfu* by James Chatto and W L Martin is a delightful description of the island through its recipes, particularly for feast days. Edward Lear's *Selected Letters* include accounts of his visits to the Ionian Islands. Botany buffs should bring *Flowers of Greece and the Aegean* by Anthony Huxley and William Taylor.

21 May and 12 December. Easter and the days dependent on the timing of Easter are according to the **Orthodox calendar** and do not often coincide with Easter in the rest of Europe. Greek tourist offices can give dates, if needed.
The Feast of St Spiridhon on 11 August is effectively a public holiday, and many shops will also be closed on the other days when St Spiridhon's remains are carried through Corfu Town, these being Palm Sunday, Easter Saturday and the first Sunday in November.

Measurements

Greece uses the metric system.

Telephones

International direct dialling is not usually a problem from Corfu. Many Greek homes do not, however, have a telephone so great use is made of **public call boxes**. Many shops and kiosks on street corners have metered phones; you simply pick up the phone, dial, and pay for the metered units at the end. Metered phones are also available in some branches of the OTE (post office).

Time

Corfu is two hours ahead of Greenwich Mean Time, one hour ahead of the rest of Western Europe, seven hours ahead of the USA's Eastern Standard Time and eight hours behind Australian New South Wales Time.

Corfu changes its clocks by one hour in spring and autumn in line with all EU countries, but this may not coincide with other parts of the world, so check if travelling near these dates.

Electricity
220AC voltage is used, with European sockets using two round pins.

Water
Water is perfectly safe to drink, though many visitors buy bottled water for personal preference. This is widely available in supermarkets and in restaurants.

Medical Services
The majority of Greek **doctors** speak at least one foreign language, usually English, as do many **pharmacists**, who are also trained to treat minor ailments and to prescribe drugs. Look for the green or red cross. There is always a pharmacy open 24 hours a day and its address should be displayed in every other pharmacy in the area (though it may only be written in Greek). Newspapers also carry notices of which pharmacists are on duty. Most towns and larger villages have a **Medical Centre**, signposted in Greek and English and normally open on weekdays from 08:00–12:00 only. Health insurance is essential, even for EU citizens who are entitled to free treatment provided that they have obtained

an EHIC card before travelling to Corfu. The main **hospital** is on Loulias Andreadi in Corfu Town, halfway between San Rocco Square and the Platytera Monastery. It has a 24-hour Casualty Department (tel: 26610 88200 / 25400). There is a clinic close to the hospital, tel: 26610 36044.

Health Hazards
There are no major health hazards on Corfu, but visitors should obviously take precautions against **sunburn**. Food upsets are not common, though some people may react against the heavy use of olive oil in cooking and on salads. If swimming, watch out for **sea urchins** in rocky areas, and occasional **jellyfish**.

Emergencies
Dial **100**, an all-purpose emergency number, or contact the local Tourist Police.

Security
Greece is one of the safest countries in the world. It may be acceptable to overcharge tourists, but few Greeks would steal from them. In busy tourist areas such as Corfu, though, your fellow tourists may not be as honest as the Corfiots, so don't leave valuables lying around. There is nowhere on Corfu where it is unsafe to walk, even late at night, although young women walking alone late at night may attract unwanted attentions, so always use common sense.

USEFUL WORDS AND PHRASES

Hello • *Yásou*
Goodbye • *Andío*
Good morning • *Kalí Méra*
Good evening • *Kalí Spéra*
How are you? • *Ti káneteh?*
Please • *Sas parakaló*
Thank You • *Sas efharisto*
Yes • *Ne*
No • *Óchi*
Excuse me • *Signómi*
Do you speak English? • *Miláteh anglika?*
Don't understand • *Dhen katalevéno*
How much is it? • *Póso káni?*
When? • *Poté?*
Where? • *Pou?*
Where is ... ? • *Poo Íne ... ?*

Hotel • *Ksendhokhio*
Post Office • *Takhidhromio*
Police • *Astinomia*
Pharmacy • *Farmakio*
Doctor • *Yatrós*
Bank • *Trapeza*
Church • *Eklisia*
Hospital • *Nosokomio*
Café • *Kafeneion*
Bus • *Leoforio*
Bus station • *Praktorio*
Restaurant • *Estiatorio*
Airport • *Aerolímenas*
Food • *Fagitó*
Saint • *Agia / Agios (Ag.)*
Church • *Eklisia*
Street • *Odos*
Square • *Platia*
Market • *Agora*
Ruins • *Eripia*
Castle • *Kastelli*
Harbour • *Limani*
Peninsula • *Khersonisos*
Gulf • *Kolpos (Kól)*
Cape / Point • *Akrotirion*
Boat • *Karavi*
Bay • *Ormos*
Beach • *Paralia*

INDEX